**Eight Visions of God's Desires
for a Covenant People**

BEFORE THE BEGINNING OF OUR WORLD

UNVEILING THE MYSTERY

Eight Visions of God's Desires
for a Covenant People

BEFORE THE BEGINNING OF OUR WORLD

UNVEILING THE MYSTERY

DON COBBLE
WITH MONA JOHNIAN

Bridge-Logos
Alachua, Florida 32615

ENDORSEMENT

My dear brother Don,

What a wonderful, awe-inspiring book you have written with Mona Johnian, your gifted spiritual mother. It runs like a pure water stream flowing from the heights of true revelation. It is fully based on the Bible and the truth that the Lord has revealed to you in His kindness and mercy, as you have walked with Him. I am so thankful to have you as a representative on our ICZC team.

May the awesomeness of this message stir many true believers to love the Lord—our very life—with all our heart and strength. Dear Don, I am thankful to God for you!

— Jan Willem van der Hoeven
   International Christian Zionist Center

Don Cobble's *Before the Beginning of Our World: Unveiling the Mystery* is an extraordinary work. Spiritually inspired and biblically based, it unveils God's marvelous plan "before the foundation of the world" and gives us great hope for the ages to come. It will bless you, encourage you, and help you realize the best is yet to come.

— Chris Mitchell, CBN journalist
   CBN News Middle East Bureau Chief, Jerusalem

FOR GOD SO LOVED THE WORLD!

The message in these pages leaves me transfixed. A veil is pulled back to reveal pre-Creation heavenly events that add a dimension to—but take nothing away from—the "thinking" of Creator God, as my limited capacity has understood it.

God is love. How remarkable to be given a richer revelation of the intensity of God's love for His Son, of which love we also have become beneficiaries.

Yes, God had a Bride in mind for His Son even from before the foundation of the world. That is *why* there was an "in the beginning."

Reading the revelations at the heart of this book, I was struck by the rich portrayal of what Don Cobble was allowed to encounter and convey. My breath caught at the scenes of glory, even as my spirit rested easy with the sense of humble reverence with which the vision scenes were laid out.

Spiritual evidences abound that we are living at the winding down of the age. In and among the Body of Messiah worldwide, tares flourish and deception is rife, as those who would glorify themselves rather than cause men to glorify God, try to tickle our ears.

Not so, I attest, the author of this work. Don is one of the finest and most self-effacing men I know. He is a faithful and accountable brother of whom it can rightly be said, "He fears the Lord."

What the Spirit has shared with him, and what he has faithfully sought to convey to us, should cause all to bow and worship the Lord.

Kol Hakavod b'shmo!—All glory to His name!

Stan Goodenough
Jerusalem Watchman
Jerusalem Newswire
Jerusalem, Israel

Bridge-Logos
Alachua, FL 32615 USA

Before the Beginning of Our World
Don Cobble with Mona Johnian

Printed in the United States of America.

Library of Congress Catalog Card Number: 2014931338
International Standard Book Number: 978-1-61036-125-5

Scripture quotations marked (KJV) are taken from the King James Version of the Bible.

Scripture quotations marked (CJB) are taken from the Complete Jewish Bible. Copyright © 1998 by David H. Stern. Published by Messianic Jewish Publishers. All rights reserved.

Scripture quotations marked (ESV) are taken from the English Standard Version of the Bible, which is published by Good News Publishers, Wheaton, IL. The ESV is adapted from the Revised Standard Version of the Bible, copyright Division of Christian Education of the National Council of Churches of Christ in the USA.

Scripture quotations marked (JUB) are taken from the Jubilee Bible © 2000, 2001, 2010 Life Sentence Publishing, Abbotsford, Wisconsin. Edited by Russell M. Stendal.

Scripture quotations marked (NIV) are taken from The Holy Bible, New International Version®, NIV® Copyright © 1973, 1978, 1984, 2011 by Biblica, Inc.™ Used by permission. All rights reserved worldwide.

Scripture quotations marked (NKJV) are taken from the New King James Version. Copyright ©1979, 1980, 1982, Thomas Nelson Inc., Publishers. Used by permission.

Scripture quotations marked (TLB) are taken from The Living Bible copyright © 1971 by Tyndale House Foundation. Used by permission of Tyndale House Publishers Inc., Carol Stream, Illinois 60188. All rights reserved.

CH 02-20-14

CONTENTS

PREFACE

SOMEWHERE I read a quote by the great English statesman, William Gladstone, who said, "No education is complete without knowledge of the Bible." As a child I was zealous to know the Bible; it was a passion that grew into maturity and filled my writing, music, and art. For the past year, as I worked on what I thought would be my legacy and last book, I began to watch Don Cobble, streaming on the Internet (The Ancient Call). I was immediately captivated by his presentation of the Book of Genesis. His depth of insight into *beginnings* was something I had never heard, read, or even thought about. After hours of conversations with him and weeks of streaming, I knew God had volunteered me to write what He had given Don. Yes, as a writer I was tired of pounding the keys, but I was in!

If I had to choose one book to explain life and destiny, it would be this amazing volume. In clear and concise language, it is a library of the brilliant magnitude of God's plans and purposes that began before there was even a world. Through eight unexpected visions, Don Cobble's theology was revolutionized into an explosion of understanding. You, too, will understand for yourself things waiting to be discovered about God and His world. It is revelation that fits every hope in your deepest heart.

What you are about to read is not only enlightening, it is thrilling beyond words. As skepticism concerning the Bible continues to increase, God is also illuminating His message in a way that challenges even the skeptics to rethink the vacuum of their unbelief.

I invite all readers—believers and skeptics—to search the Scriptures and see if these things be true, just as the early Christians searched.
— Mona Johnian, coauthor

INTRODUCTION
Before Our Six-Day Creation

EVERY morning I take a circular walk among the trees in the wooded area where I live. As a teacher of the Bible, it is a good time to pray and meditate on the subject I am developing. On this particular morning I was working on a series called, "The Seed," from the Book of Genesis ("In the beginning God created the heavens . . ."). And this is where I was stopped dead in my tracks. It was a place I would stay for several weeks, pondering what I was hearing and seeing. That day represented a paradigm shift, a turning point in my understanding of Creation, that would revolutionize my theology and open scriptural truths I had never considered.

Before I share the visions, allow me to clarify with the following: I am not a person for whom supernatural events are commonplace. In fact, I have had only one other similar experience, which I put into a small book called, *Does My Life Count For Something?* This account was based on an unexpected vision of the judgment seat of Christ, and the believer's reward.

On the first day of the eight visions, perfectly aware of my natural surroundings, I was engaged in deep thought when suddenly my attention was drawn to a scene in heaven. I could actually see movement, hear the conversations and understand what was going on.

When the scene finally disappeared, I was visibly affected and could hardly think about it without tears. I didn't know it then, but it was only the beginning. In the days that followed, God was waiting for me to join Him for more of the unveilings.

The simplest explanation for what these unveiled scenes were like is *dreams*. Imagine having dreams while you are wide awake; you know where you are, yet you also know that what you are hearing and seeing are events beyond the natural.

Admittedly, such an experience is mystical, but it is not mysticism. "Mysticism" means experiencing the spirit realm outside of Scripture, whereas "mystical" refers to experiences that occur within the context of the Bible, such as those the prophets, apostles, and other believers have had and recorded, until the present.

The nature of these experiences concerned me. I didn't question if I were really seeing and hearing these things, but were they from God? I knew that the only way to know for sure was to test them by the written word of God. The search didn't take long to substantiate my visions in both the Old and New Testament Scriptures.

Secret Wisdom

Paul wrote to the young church:

> Among the mature we do impart wisdom,
> although it is not a wisdom of this age, or of the
> rulers of this age, who are doomed to pass away.
> But we impart a secret and hidden wisdom of God,
> which God decreed before the ages for our glory.
> (1 Corinthians 2:6–7, ESV)

Since God decreed secret and hidden wisdom before the ages, the purpose of my visions is to bring greater understanding to the mysteries hidden in the Word of God that are being unveiled today. The secret, hidden wisdom of God was designed to bring mankind into God's glory. This is the glory you will discover in this book.

When the Creator speaks declarations, they *become!* His full intentions have yet to be revealed. God has secrets He calls mysteries. Today, they are being given greater clarity.

God spoke decrees *before* the creation of the natural realm as it is recorded in Scripture. Before our world came into existence, the Kingdom of Heaven was created, designed, established, populated with angels, and fully functioning. As I now understand it, God's kingdom was the first to be created. He populated it with angels, who would serve to assist Him in accomplishing His will and purposes for our six-day Creation.

God's words are not empty. From the beginning, the fullness of His plans has been veiled in part. He reveals things that are already here, yet hidden for the future. As the prophet Daniel said, "There is a God in heaven who reveals mysteries" (Daniel 2:28, ESV).

God's people have not always gotten their timing right, and they have sometimes misread the prophets, but this does not alarm God, nor has He changed one word of all He has purposed. After countless ages, His hidden wisdom is right on schedule.

The Tactical Sovereign

God is a tactical Sovereign. He has no equal. Once understood, the beginning of His plan is matchless. His method for unfolding its component parts is like a general's strategy. The time for releasing a hidden mystery comes at the specific moment it is due to appear on the stage of engagement, and He uses whomever He wills to carry out His plan.

The Format

This book contains the eight visions in Section One, including commentary about the meaning of the visions. Section Two consists of seven chapters in which I summarize the scriptural verification and understanding that I have received from these remarkable encounters.

In this last section of the book, I will share some of the insights that continue to unfold, as I study and teach the messages of *Before the Beginning of our World*. The response I am receiving is the same from culture to culture and country to country: understanding the beginnings fills in the missing pieces of the mysteries of life.

The Bible is not only the most printed book ever, it is the most advanced book in print. Unveiled, its truths dispel the spiritual confusion that keeps skewing the reality of the biblical God, and His purpose for creation.

SECTION ONE

Vision One

GOD, THE SPIRIT REALM, THE CITY OF ANGELS

He [Abraham] looked for a city which has foundations,
whose builder and maker is God. (Hebrews II:I0, JUB)

I N a panoramic view, as though I were looking down
from a mountaintop, I saw a great city. In style, it looked
like a thirteenth-century kingdom city here on earth. The
architecture was similar to the ancient period of cathedrals,
ribbed vaults, great archways, and gatehouses. It looked somewhat
like a monarchical kingdom, the major difference being that this
city was inhabited solely by angels who operated as a functioning
society. I could not determine the specific jobs of the angels, but
all work was manual. No machines were being used in this city.
Carts that appeared to be made of wood were the vehicles used
to transport things, and the only modes of transportation I saw
were horses and foot travel. Every angel was actively engaged in
daily life.

The overwhelming impression of the city was a luminous
aura; a soft light emanated from everything that existed, enhanced by
faint pastel colors. The angels, the buildings, the animals, everything
in the city cast a glow. Besides the luminescence, the city had the
vitality of a thriving metropolis. Inexplicably, I knew I was looking
at the City of God.

God's Throne

At the highest point of the City of God is where The Holy One dwells. He is the center of everything going on. I did not see the invisible God, but I heard Him. I did, however, see His Presence; He dwells in light and He himself is also light. The Word is true: "He wraps himself with light as with a garment" (Psalm 104:2, NIV). "God is light, and in him is no darkness at all" (1 John 1:5, NKJV).

Have you ever wondered where God was before He created everything? Peering into the God who is light, I understood that from eternity, there was only God. Before God created anything He was not somewhere, He was all that existed *everywhere*.

Because we exist in a realm of space and darkness, we tend to picture God, before Creation, all alone in a vast sea of this same darkness. In reality, God, who is Light, has always existed in the fullness and brightness of His own Light and Life. At no time has God ever been in darkness. From the position of light, He spoke, and the created realm of the highest heavens, the kingdom, and the civilization of angels came to be. It is a marvel that mortals can even think on the level of such glory, much less experience and write about it.

The Hebrew prophets and the New Testament apostles Paul and John, along with men and women after the scriptural canon was closed, have documented experiences of the spiritual realm similar to the one that I was suddenly viewing, yet I remained puzzled by what it all meant. This is when understanding began to push back the boundaries of my mind with the simple example of an egg.

The Egg

But will God indeed dwell with men on the
earth? Behold heaven and the heaven of heavens
cannot contain you. (2 Chronicles 6:18, NKJV)

Think of the whole of creation as being in the shape of an egg, lying in the hand of God. The shell of the egg is creation's boundaries. The highest heavens are the white of the egg; the yolk is where God

2

placed our sacred universe. The Creator is outside His creation, yet He chose to enter into His creation, where He promises to dwell with us one day.

The fact that God has chosen to enter into and be known by His creation, is one of the most outstanding characteristics that distinguishes Him from all other religions and their gods.

The highest heavenly kingdom was created in the perfect light. Yet, the created kingdom is less than the Eternal Light who reigns over the kingdom. The created is always less than the creator, just as a print is always less than the original. God is transcendent over all.

I have suggested the egg image to give you a visual of what I saw and understood to be the Kingdom of Heaven, and the city in which God's presence is manifested. Yet God and only God exists outside His heavens.

Pre-Earth Creation

Bearing in mind that I was seeing only what happened *before* the six-day creation of planet Earth, this first vision was revolutionary. I came to understand that the angels have always mirrored God's emotions and will. Jesus said, "There will be . . . joy in heaven over one sinner that repents" (Luke 15:7, NIV). This means angels have a full range of emotions.

They also form choirs. At the birth of Messiah, a great angel made an announcement, accompanied by a choir of angels:

> . . . the *Sh'khinah* of Adonai shone about
> them [the shepherds], but the angel said to them,
> "Don't be afraid, because I am here announcing
> to you Good News that will bring great joy to all
> the people." . . . Suddenly, along with the angel
> was a vast army from heaven praising God.
> "In the highest heaven, Glory to God! And on
> earth, peace among people of good will!"
> (Luke 2:9–10, 13–14, CJB)

Angel Languages

Angels are personal intelligent spirits with superhuman communication skills. Paul said, "Though I speak with the tongues [languages] of men and of angels . . ." (1 Corinthians 13:1, NKJV). As you will see in the next vision, angels are multilingual. They speak in numerous angel-languages, yet they also speak in the language of human beings. When Gabriel announced to Mary that she would carry the Son of God, he spoke in Hebrew/Aramaic (see Luke 2). But men can also speak in the language of angels.

According to the Apostle Paul, who was versed in several human languages, he sometimes prayed or sang in the language of angels, enabled by the Holy Spirit:

> If I speak in the tongues of men and of angels. . . . There are doubtless many different languages in the world, and none is without meaning. . . . I will sing praise with my spirit but I will sing with my mind also. (1 Corinthians 13:1–14:10, 15, ESV)

Free Will

Angels have free will, which is subject to moral parameters—they can choose to obey or disobey. Those who went outside their original design, committing sexual perversions with human beings, received swift judgment:

> And the angels that did not keep within their original authority, but abandoned their proper sphere, he has kept in darkness, bound with everlasting chains for the Judgment of the Great Day. And S'dom and Amora . . . following a pattern like theirs, committing sexual sins and perversions, lie exposed as a warning of the everlasting fire awaiting those who must undergo punishment. (Jude 6–7, CJB)

Angels are less than Jesus (see Hebrews 1:4), yet they execute divine assignments at high levels, as well as simple assignments here on earth: "Are they not all ministering spirits sent forth to minister for those who will inherit salvation?" (Hebrews 1:14, NKJV).

Angels are glorious: "For whoever is ashamed of Me and My words, of him the Son of Man will be ashamed when He comes in His own glory, and in His Father's, and of the holy angels" (Luke 9:26, NKJV).

Loss of the Holy

As the first inhabitants created for the Holy City, it only seems fitting that angels are called "holy." Holy angels have eternal existence. "Neither can they [resurrected people] die any more: for they are equal unto the angels" (Luke 20:36, KJV). Yet, we will see in graphic description how one-third of heaven's angels fell with Lucifer and lost their place in heaven. Places with God can be lost, including powerful-but-created angels.

A truth I would see repeated in the visions is the fact that although angels live in the City of God, they are not omnipotent (all-powerful), or omniscient (all-knowing). Concerning the return of Jesus, Mark wrote, "But of that day and that hour knoweth no man, no, not the angels which are in heaven" (Mark 13:32, KJV).

Angels were created by the Word, and should not be worshiped: "Let no man beguile you . . . in a voluntary humility [cults] and worshipping of angels" (Colossians 2:16, KJV). In fact, angels attend church services in order to learn the mysteries of God's plans (see Ephesians 3:10).

Directed only by God, angels give assistance, protection, guidance, and provision. They appear in dreams, receive departed spirits, bring answers to prayer, and provide hundreds of other helps to the saints. Here is an example of what they do:

On a snowy evening in Connecticut, imbedded in four lanes of fast-moving traffic, two of my family were in a small Volkswagen when it began to hydroplane. The car suddenly spun around and they were going backward down the interstate at 60 miles an hour with absolutely no control. They were now *facing* the four lanes of traffic with which they had been traveling. On one side of the four lanes was a jagged rock wall; on the other side was a dark ravine. One of them suddenly cried out in a loud voice, "Jesus! Jesus! Jesus!" The car suddenly came to an abrupt halt—sitting on the grass, headed in the right direction! Angels are swift and powerful agents that respond instantly to the voice of God.

Now I understand that before there was a globe, there was definitely a kingdom realm, a fully functioning empire with a civilization of angels, where God is sovereign. This kingdom preceded the foundation of Earth. "Come, you blessed of My Father, inherit the kingdom prepared for you from the foundation of the world" (Matthew 25:34, NKJV).

The End of Vision One

FURTHER COMMENTARY:
THE WORLD OF SPIRIT AND ANGELS

The word "kingdom" in Greek is *basileia,* and it means a royal foundation of power. The power of the kingdom of heaven is foundational to the rest of creation. It supersedes even the greatest powers of the universe, yet its power is available to mere mortals: Jesus said,

> Fear not little flock, for it is your Father's good
> pleasure to give you the kingdom. . . . Provide
> yourselves with moneybags that do not grow
> old, with a treasure in the heavens that does not
> fail. . . . For where your treasure is there will your
> heart be also. (Luke 12:32–34, ESV)

The Spirit Realm and the Angels

The Apostle Paul said, "I pray God your whole spirit and soul and body be preserved blameless unto the coming of the Lord"(1 Thessalonians 5:23, KJV). Human beings are both natural and spiritual. We are spirit, living in a body, with a soul (mind, will, emotion). But, unlike angels who can manifest in both the natural and spirit realms, we are confined to natural bodies in a natural world, at this point in God's plan.

The fact of the existence of various realms of creation is established in Paul's statement: "That at the name of Jesus every knee should bow, of things in heaven, and on earth, and under the earth; and that every tongue should confess that Jesus Christ is Lord, to the glory of God the Father" (Philippians 2:10–11, KJV). In heaven, earth, and under the earth—throughout all realms of existence—the visible and the invisible, the seen and the unseen, all peoples, all angels, all creatures will one day acknowledge that the one God, the Creator is the source of life. Even in the lowest hell, people will realize that for love of mankind and creation, the eternal God manifested himself as a human being and surrendered His natural life to restore a fallen world.

Biblical history records that the invisible God, Who is Spirit, has manifested himself in many ways. For Israel He became a cloud, a pillar of fire, and a rock that produced water in the desert, but when His Word took the form of man, God became naturally visible. The natural visible Son of God, who died and who was resurrected, became the visible Redeemer.

According to the Apostle Paul, though God is invisible, He has never been unperceivable to mankind, as we tend to think:

> For the truth about God is known to them
> instinctively; God has put this knowledge in their
> hearts. Since earliest times men have seen the earth
> and sky and all God made, and have known of
> His existence and great eternal power. (Romans
> 1:18–20, TLB)

Everything, visible and invisible, was created by Him. Many visible things are a copy of the true pattern of invisible realities.

In their celebration at the birth of Jesus, the angel choirs filling the heavens must have been beyond any choral sound ever to exist on earth, and their only audience were simple shepherds whose names have never even been researched. Yet, their eternal song continues to resound in every generation of "those who have ears to hear what the spirit is saying."

Vision Two
ARCHANGELS PREPARE FOR AN ANNOUNCEMENT

IN my second vision, I saw the archangels Michael, Gabriel, and Lucifer standing with their backs to me, facing the presence of God. They were being instructed to prepare the angelic hosts for an announcement. It was my understanding that God was about to decree something unprecedented to the heavenly population. It concerned the imminent unveiling of His creation plans, although no angel knew this, including the archangels.

Before they were called into the Presence, I had seen Michael, Gabriel, and Lucifer out among the angelic population, each in the area of his particular dominion or command. When the call came from God, it was not audible, meaning no one heard His call except the angel to whom it was directed. Although they were all addressed at the same time, they did not know the other had been summoned, until the three arrived in God's presence. I saw Michael respond to his call and prepare to report.

This is when the scene changed and the three of them stood facing the Presence. Suspended above and looking down into this scene, I not only saw what was going on, I heard what was being said. Even though I was positioned at a distance, my view allowed me to see the unapproachable light in which God dwells. If this light was total God, I cannot say. ". . . who alone has immortality, dwelling in unapproachable light, whom no man has seen or can see, to whom be honor and everlasting power. Amen" (1 Timothy 6:16, NKJV).

I was above and behind the three archangels. Michael was to my left, Gabriel was standing in the middle, and Lucifer was to my right. There was no interaction among the three archangels as they stood before God; it was only God to individual angel, and individual angel to Him.

The Visible Presence of God

The visible presence of God, as I saw Him, was one of fire and light, gently swirling in the form of a whirlwind as if in slow motion; it was awesome in the truest sense of the word. The fiery swirl was about fifteen feet wide and I saw no top. I did hear a faint hum from the movement of the light. The color of the presence of God was bright white light with a faint blue tint—the color of a welder's arc.

This swirling light was a fire, but I had no sense of intense heat. The voice of God came forth out of this light with strength and force. You did not just hear His voice, you felt it. As the Bible records, His Presence demands reverence and awe: "Therefore, since we are receiving a kingdom that cannot be shaken, let us be thankful, and so worship God acceptably with reverence and awe, for our 'God is a consuming fire'" (Hebrews 12:28–29, NIV).

Surrounding the presence of God were three walls of light. Each wall was of the same color as the light of the invisible God, but not the same intensity. There was the inner circle surrounded by the second and then the third wall. I understood that you could neither see nor hear through these walls of light. Though they were only about thirty feet high, I knew there was no way through any of them except by invitation from God. I could only see what was going on in the inner circle with the archangels; I did not see what was between the other two curtain-walls of light. I also did not see how the angels came in or went out.

In the presence of God, I heard Him say to the archangels: *"Have the angels prepare themselves, for I will address the hosts with a declaration of unprecedented proportion!"* This declaration was concerning the creation of our universe and God's purpose for mankind.

⋙ The End of Vision Two ⋙

FURTHER COMMENTARY:
THE PRE-SIX-DAY CREATION

Prior to the visions, it was my understanding that the "evening and morning of the first day" recorded in Genesis was the beginning of creation. However, I now understand that this was the first day of the six-day creation of our universe, it was not the beginning of God's works. Before the first day of our universe, God had created the heavens, with a kingdom, a civilization of angels, a city, and many other things.

This creation period, referred to in Scripture as "before the foundations of the Earth were laid," is what I mean by the pre-six-day creation.

There are numerous biblical references of events that occurred before the laying of the foundation of Earth and before the six-day creation story that is recorded in Genesis. The following is a partial list of some of these pre-creation events:

1. **Heaven was created before the earth:** "In *the beginning* God created the heavens and the earth" (Genesis 1:1, KJV, emphasis added).

2. **The Son had glory with the Father before the six-day Creation:** "I glorified you on earth by finishing the work you gave me to do. Now, Father, glorify me alongside yourself. Give me the same glory I had with you *before the world existed*" (John 17:4–5, CJB, emphasis added).

3. **There were angels before creation of Earth:** "Where were you when *I founded the earth*. . . . when the morning stars sang together, and all the sons of God [angels] shouted

for joy?" (Job 38:4, 7, CJB, emphasis added).

4. **Blood redemption was established before the six-day Creation:** ". . . the book of life of the Lamb slain from the foundation of the world" (Revelation 13:8, KJV).

5. **Purpose and Grace were given before the six-day Creation:** "Accept your share in suffering disgrace for the sake of the Good News. God will give you the strength for it . . . because of his own purpose and the grace which he gave to us who are united with the Messiah Yeshua. He did this *before the beginning of time,* but made it public only now through the appearing of our Deliverer" (2 Timothy 1:8–9, CJB, emphasis added).

6. **Eternal life was appropriated pre-six-day Creation:** "In the Messiah [Jesus], He chose us in love *before the creation of the universe* to be holy and without defect in his presence" (Ephesians 1:4, CJB, emphasis added). ". . . God, who does not lie, promised that life *before the beginning of time"* (Titus 1:2, CJB, emphasis added).

7. **A kingdom was prepared for mankind before the foundations of the world:** "Then the King will say to those on his right, 'Come, you whom my Father has blessed, take your inheritance, the Kingdom prepared for you *from the founding of the world'"* (Matthew 25:34, CJB, emphasis added).

8. **Works for the believers were planned before their creation:** ". . . his works have been in existence *since the founding of the universe"* (Hebrews 4:3, CJB, emphasis added). Paul said, "God, *who picked me out before I was born and called me by his grace,* chose to reveal his Son to me, so that I might announce him to the Gentiles" (Galatians 1:15, CJB, emphasis added). "The work is to make fully known the message from God, *the secret hidden for generations, for ages,* but now made clear to the people he has set apart for himself . . . how great among the Gentiles is

the glorious richness of this secret . . . Messiah is united with you people. In that rests your hope of glory!" (Colossians 1:25-27, CJB, emphasis added).

9. **Believers' names were written in the Book of Life pre-six-day Creation:** "The people living on earth whose names have not been written in the Book of Life *since the founding of the world* will be astounded" (Revelation 17:8, CJB, emphasis added).

10. **The foundation of the earth preceded the creation of the Earth:** "Where were you when I laid the foundations?" (Job 38:4, KJV).

11. **There was a fully functioning tabernacle in heaven, with a High Priest, before Creation:** "We do have such a *cohen gadol* [High Priest] as has been described. And he does sit at the right hand of *HaG'dulah* [God] in heaven. There he serves in the Holy Place, that is in the true Tent of Meeting [Tabernacle], *Adonai* [God]. For every *cohen gadol* is appointed to offer both gifts and sacrifices . . . but what they are serving is only a copy and shadow of the heavenly original; for when Moshe was about to erect the Tent, God warned him, see to it that you make everything according to the pattern you were shown on the mountain . . . But now the work *Yeshua* [Jesus] has been given to do is far superior to theirs" *(Hebrews 8:1–6, CJB).*

12. **Mysteries were kept secret from the foundations.** Paul wrote: "Now to God, who can strengthen you, according to my Good News, in harmony with the revelation of the *secret truth* which is the proclamation of Yeshua the Messiah [Jesus], *kept hidden in silence for ages and ages,* but manifested now through prophetic writings, in keeping with the command of God the Eternal and communicated to all Gentiles to promote in them trust-grounded obedience—to the only wise God, through Yeshua [Jesus] the Messiah, be the glory forever and ever! Amen" (Romans 16:25–27, CJB, emphasis added).

13. **Parables revealed pre-six-day Creation truths:** "I will open my mouth in parables, I will say what has been hidden since the creation of the universe" (Matthew 13:34, CJB). "We are communicating a secret wisdom from God which has been hidden until now but which, before history began, God had decreed would bring us glory" (1 Corinthians 2:7, CJB).

The Temple in Heaven

The thought of God is mysterious to human beings because we have no natural comparison, but this does not mean God has not revealed generous evidence in creation about what He is like. By looking at the tabernacle in the wilderness, we can know exactly what the temple from which God rules and is worshiped looks like. This is perhaps the most obvious revelation God has made of himself to mankind. It is visible proof that the Creator is ruler of all, but at the same time He desires to communicate with and be known intimately by all. False mystical religions say God cannot be known. The tabernacle in the wilderness was God's meeting place with Israel.

In the wilderness God commanded Israel to take the things He had provided, dedicate everything to Him, and then build Him a tabernacle where He would come and meet with them. In essence, this invitation was like a king who sent a blueprint of His palace, with orders to build an exact replica where he would come and meet with the people, provide and gift them with every imaginable blessing of his eternal kingdom. The ability to meet with God personally and intimately is the single greatest invitation of life. It is the foundation of all of the mysteries written in Scripture, inspired by the Breath of God. But what kind of Creator would go to such lengths to have a relationship with His creation? This is the question for true "critical thinkers."

Vision Three
ARCHANGELS MEET WITH CAPTAINS

I N the third vision I was suddenly there, observing the three archangels who had just been in the presence of God. For the first time I was seeing them from the front.

First, Michael the archangel appeared. He was an impressive muscular, gladiator-like warrior, with a strap across his chest at an angle. His skirt was knee-length and he wore a brilliant headband. From Scripture, I recognized him as the prince who stands for Israel (see Daniel 10:20).

Next, Gabriel the archangel appeared. He was well-built and also wore a brilliant headband, but in his dress and demeanor he looked less like a warrior than Michael. Both wore sandals with straps to the knees.

Last, Lucifer the archangel appeared. He too looked like a warrior, but he was much more decorated than Michael or Gabriel. The stones on his garment and sandals were continually flashing brilliant lights. When he released praise or worship, his stones lit up even more. The multicolored rays from the stones appeared to come from a light within each gem, and their beams shot out in lightning-like brilliance. In appearance, he was the most glorious of the three archangels, or of any angel I saw.

The Scene Changed

The scene changed, and I was looking down into a round room. It was about thirty feet across. Each of the three archangels had four strong, warrior-captains under his personal command, and they always accompanied him, except when the archangels went into the presence of God. The captains would wait for them in the round conference room nearby, seated at a large round table, where instructions would be issued after the archangels' meeting with God.

In this scene, the three archangels suddenly appeared in the conference room to meet with their captains. Each archangel was standing beside his door, indicating that each had his own entrance. The doorways were pointed at the top and appeared to be made of heavy wood, resembling the style of doors in an ancient castle.

The three archangels conferred with their captains, instructing them to spread the following word: At a set time (not measurable in human terms), "All angels are to be present at the base of the holy Mountain of the Lord. God is going to deliver a declaration!"

None of the angels knew the details of the declaration to be delivered, but all were visibly excited. I understood that most of the angelic population had never seen the Presence, nor heard the voice of God.

A Description of the Heavenly Mountain of God

The heavenly temple mount was not like an imposing Mt. Everest, whose summit point cannot be seen, but the top of the mountain where God dwells could be seen from all directions. The Mountain of the Lord is not a figure of speech; it is an actual place in the City of God, located at the highest point of heaven. It is a mountaintop surrounded by walls of light.

Each angel has the ability to hear from God personally in a way that others do not hear the conversation—which is also true for human beings. Be it angel or human, communication with God is a personal matter, and even in the presence of others, a spiritual exchange with God is private. Scripture gives many accounts when God spoke and others sensed His Presence, but neither saw nor heard anything. Any person who knows God understands this spiritual transaction.

The prophet Daniel was on the banks of the Tigris River (in modern Iran) when he had a visit from Gabriel. "Only I, Daniel, saw the vision; the men who were with me did not see the vision; however, a great trembling came over them; so they rushed to hide themselves" (Daniel 10:7, CJB).

Note: Whether or not man realizes it, the voice and will of God affects all creation individually. God is often the source of baffling turns in a life, which will only be understood years later.

 The End of Vision Three

FURTHER COMMENTARY:
GOD'S DESIRE FOR RELATIONSHIP

(I consider the following notes to be of particular importance, as they address the motivations of the God who set up such elaborate plans. First He builds a kingdom with a magnificent city to surround His throne, He creates a civilization of powerful angels to assist Him, and then He commissions His most powerful angelic statesmen to assemble billions of angels for a history-birthing declaration.)

Although God lacks nothing, inherent in His *Being* are desires that He cannot remain alone and fulfill. God warned Israel that their unfaithfulness to Him was the root cause of their troubles. He said plainly, "For I desire steadfast love and not sacrifice, the knowledge of God rather than burnt offerings" (Hosea 6:6, ESV).

In other words, God desires to be known and loved. God is building a kingdom and He wants people with whom He can relate, people who *choose* (because He gave them freedom of will) to be transformed into His image, whose character is based on knowledge of and desire for Him.

The Love of the Burning Flame

The God-Creator, who dwells enthroned in the Holy Place in a real kingdom, has desires that moved Him to make the initial sacrifice of genuine love. The gentle whirlwind that Job saw, and that I saw, had such desire for loving relationships that He literally sacrificed the life of His Son to gain eternal life for His creation.

Have you ever wished you had not been born? Think again. You were born because God desired it, with a pure desire that would satisfy both His heart and yours. Even when Israel was steeped in sin and their love toward God had grown cold, He approached them: "Efrayim, what should I do to you? Y'hudah, what should I do to you? For your 'faithful love' is like a morning cloud, like dew that disappears quickly" (Hosea 6:4, CJB). Ephraim and Judah were hardly out of Egypt before their faithfulness to God evaporated. They kept the ritual, but in their hearts they were unfaithful covenant-breakers. God requires genuine relationship-commitment: "Hear O Israel, the Lord our God, He is One. . . . You shall have no other gods beside me" (see Deuteronomy 6:4; Exodus 20:3).

The promise to Abraham was the *Seed*. The natural seed of Abraham was Israel, but the spiritual seed was Messiah, the Word of God in human form, looking for the heart:

> In the beginning was the Word and the
> Word was with God, and the Word was God. . . .
> And the word became flesh and dwelt among us,
> and we have seen his glory, glory as of the only
> Son from the Father, full of grace and truth."
> (John 1:1, 14, ESV)

With the visions from my walks stirring in my thoughts, I weighed the "worship" of the church today—the ritual offerings, the small tributes we utter under our breath, the frequent effort to weigh our good deeds against the heart of the Burning Flame that exists from eternity—and I realized how little we truly understand about our

Creator and purpose that moves Him to act in creation.

The veil has been pulled back. The mystery of God's identity is no longer hidden. Almost two thousand years ago, during a conversation with a woman at a well in Samaria, this secret mystery was brought out into the open: "The woman said to him [Jesus], 'I know that Messiah is coming (he who is called Christ). When he comes, he will tell us all things.' Jesus said to her, 'I who speak to you am he'" (John 4:25–26, ESV).

This is the depth of commitment the Father made to fulfill His desire for a relationship based of love. He committed; we commit. He gave His life; we give our life. And together, we enjoy the priceless gift of Life in His eternal kingdom.

Vision Four
SPONTANEOUS WORSHIP ERUPTS

I N Vision Four, what I saw took place among the general population of the angelic hosts. In this scene the three archangels were together, like commanders in the field among their soldiers, when they began discussing the greatness of God in anticipation of what He was going to decree. There appeared to be an affectionate relationship among the three. As they continued talking, emotions began to rise and Lucifer began to escalate his glorification of the Lord. Gabriel and Michael looked at each other as if to say, "Here we go!"

As Lucifer erupted into the worship and praise of God, the gems in his robe were beaming! His voice was similar to God's, in that you *felt* it. His worship created a spontaneous ripple effect. As his volume began to rise and resonate you could not only hear him, but also feel the anointing. The power of the anointing elevated Lucifer into worship that caused Gabriel and Michael to join him unreservedly. And with that, a wave of praise was released throughout the kingdom that spread from angel to angel all the way through the bright realms of heaven and into the glorious heights of ecstasy.

It was then I understood why Lucifer is believed to have been the worship leader in heaven. Lucifer's anointing drew praise and worship to God that would increase exponentially, and it could happen anywhere, spontaneously. It explained his beautiful, gem-studded garment and sandals. It enlightened me to the fact of the absolute importance of the worship of God. I understood that spontaneous worship is appropriate throughout creation.

(Note: This applies to earthlings as well. Even if a person is in a place where audible worship is not allowed, the soul and spirit can worship from within. Worship is the lifeline to God. It draws the life of God into any situation, bringing His strength, comfort and wisdom to the worshiper.)

As word of an impending announcement spread, great excitement erupted throughout the realm—common angels were going to be allowed to hear from the manifest presence of God! Common angels knew what God was like only by the reports of the archangels who had been in His Presence. Their anticipation of hearing from God directly again confirmed that angels are not omniscient just because they are spirit beings who live in the Kingdom of God. Angels, like human beings, have to *learn* what they know. Although they all reverence the magnitude of God, most, maybe none, have ever seen behind the veils of light. Neither being in heaven nor knowing God grants omniscience (all knowledge).

Let me also add that I never once interacted with any of these visions. I was nothing more than a greatly privileged observer.

 The End of Vision Four

FURTHER COMMENTARY:
GIVING WORSHIP TO GOD

We might say the first heavenly pattern for organized worship can be found in the desert, when Israel was migrating from Egypt back to Canaan. It began with a call from God for voluntarily giving for the building of a tabernacle of worship, which brings up the question, "Why do we give verbal homage and material things to God in heaven, who needs nothing?" But as you will see, the gift is not the point; it is the attitude of the heart that adds value. What God desires is not our words or our things. Jesus hit the nail on the head by saying, "Where your treasure is there will your heart be also" (Matthew 6:21, KJV).

A person's relationship to his or her things is a window to the soul. A stingy heart is despicable to a generous God. A heart that prefers to hold on to things that will rust and decay, a heart that is afraid to give with glad release, a heart that puts satisfaction of the senses above spiritual maturity, is not a heart that pleases the God who created and owns all things: "For the world is mine, and the fullness thereof" (Psalm 50:12, KJV).

Worship is giving back to God what He first gave to you—and that is life. Worship is the lifeline to the Source of life. Giving to God cannot be overstated. Creation is beautiful; Earth is a scientific dream; mankind in God's image is a mystery. But nothing that exists is as important as God. Without Him, nothing has any lasting significance. Everything, including our very breath, belongs to God. Worship lays our heart open to Him.

I have been in the Middle Eastern desert on numerous occasions, during both war and peace. There is no place more forbidding on the planet. Yet, it was in the desert that God asked Israel to give something called a "heave offering" for the building of the tabernacle.

The Heave Offering

And what was the heave offering? It was a free-will offering given to God, not grudgingly or by force, but joyfully from the heart. Moses wrote, "So they came, both men and women. All who were of a willing heart brought brooches and earrings and signet rings and armlets, all sorts of gold objects, every man dedicating an offering of gold to the Lord" (Exodus 35:22, ESV).

And how does this connect with my visions of a God whose throne is so distant we could never reach His sphere, even with a futuristic space launcher? The point is: worship is not a function but an active spiritual relationship. The God who is life, is not disconnected from the people and things He made.

Because of the influence of the ancient Gnostic heresy, according to which creation was considered evil and temporary, it is hard to envision a God who considers natural and material things important. But if we take the time to read the components of the heave offering we will get a more accurate view of how God relates to His creation.

The Heave Offering Contained:

1. **Precious Metals and Materials:** gold; silver; brass; textiles of blue/violet, purple, scarlet, *byssus* (a linen weave that surpasses anything known today), goats' hair, ramskins, badger skins.

2. **Acacia wood**

3. **Oil**

4. **Spices:** myrrh, cinnamon, sweet calamus. Also **spices for the incense** (see Exodus 30:34–38): stacte, onycha, galbanum, frankincense

5. **Precious Stones:** sardis (brownish red), topaz (yellow/red), emerald (green), carbuncle (red garnet), sapphire (deep blue), diamond (sparkling white), amber (yellow), agate (blue), amethyst (violet), beryl (greenish yellow), onyx (bright yellow), jasper (pure and clear)

But why should people give something they may need, to a God who has everything? Why would God be interested in natural things when there are so many dire needs in the world?

As we will see in Vision Five, the God of the Bible is more real and more closely related to this world than we have allowed ourselves to think. The Creator who gave man existence also made all of the raw materials we see and live with every day. God is not a god of religious mysticism who hides somewhere in space. God made the horses I saw the archangels riding in His kingdom. He made the precious metals, wood, oil, spices, and gemstones used to decorate His house, as well as the people of His house here on earth. "You also as lively stones, are built up a spiritual house, an holy priesthood, to offer up spiritual sacrifices, acceptable to God by Jesus Christ" (1 Peter 2:5, KJV). You are a beautiful gem in the eyes of God. You are a gold mine, a silver chest, a plot of fertile soil. You are a treasure! In Malachi 3:17, He calls us His "jewels."

The Profile

The heave offering (the gifts of the willing worshiper) also reveals another powerful truth: Every offering for the building of the tabernacle was *a profile of the coming Redeemer and His work*.

Once the gifts were given to God, the offerings were transformed into altars, spices, and anointing oils, which typify the *sacrifice of Jesus*. The gold and oil provided the lamp and light of Jesus; the acacia wood was used to build the Ark of the Presence of the Father among His people.

In mystery form, the heave offering tells humanity that every life and possession is a gift from God that is to be dedicated back to God on the altar of sacrifice. Regardless of how small or large a person's wealth, talents, or skills, when they are dedicated to God, they comprise a spiritual treasure.

This indicates that we should not give simply because of someone's need; rather we dedicate all to God and we give as He directs. Remember, God desires relationships, and the gift of one's whole heart is the offering God is seeking. From that relationship will come responsible giving, common grace for humanity, and anointed labor, praise, and worship worthy of the Father.

Vision Five
THE DAY OF ANNOUNCEMENT

IN the fifth vision, I saw and heard God's decree to the heavenly kingdom concerning His intentions to create our world—all celestial bodies including planet Earth. On this particular planet, mankind would be created in God's very own likeness—the nearest to God's image without being God—and they, of their own free will, would receive and return the love of God.

Everything about this gathering was exceedingly bright, with innumerable hosts of angels waiting at the base of the Mountain of God. The voice of God began to resound from behind the curtains of light, through which no one could pass. The curtains opened ever so slightly as God spoke.

(For a biblical view of what happened on this day read Job 38 in its entirety, which I had not done before my visual encounters. It begins by confirming the description of God as I saw Him in the vision: "Then God answered Job out of the whirlwind. . . ." This is what I saw, a gently swirling whirlwind. "Where were you when I laid the foundation of the earth? . . . Who determined its measurements. . . . or who stretched the line upon it? On what were its bases sunk, or who laid its cornerstone?" [Job 38:4–7, ESV].)

The Omni Theater

From the wooded area where I was standing, I watched this scene unfold in amazement. Nothing I have ever seen was so glorious. When God spoke, He began by declaring His plans to create a universe with planets, stars, and celestial bodies. As He was making these declarations, the heavens became like a gigantic Omni theater, filled with visual images of the things He had uttered. Suns, moons, stars, and celestial bodies sparkled like diamonds before the angels.

In that environment, the angels raised their hands and began to shout in awe at the inexplicable glory, until the entire heavens were filled with brilliant lights and angelic sounds of rejoicing.

Man

Then God announced the unimaginable. In the midst of this magnificent display of celestial lights, God declared: "And I am going to make MAN!–a race of beings created in My image, who will inhabit the Earth!" And with those words, accompanied by stunning visuals, shouts broke out among the angels into an even greater dimension.

All Nations

God then began to make numerous declarations of the things He would do with this wonderful creation of humanity. In short clips, I saw thousands upon thousands of people from all nationalities with their hands raised, shouting praises to God in their national languages. There were languages of Hallelujahs from horizon to horizon. I saw Africans, Asians, Indians, Europeans, North and South Americans, Middle Easterners, and more–people of every language and all nations–with their hands raised in worship, shouting praises to God.

At that moment, Lucifer escalated the celebrations with a voice that boomed beyond the sound of all other worshipers, which lifted everything into a sonorous pinnacle of praise, similar to what is recorded in the Psalms:

> Praise ye the Lord.
> Praise ye the Lord from the heavens:
> praise him in the heights.
> Praise ye him, all his angels, praise ye him,
> all his hosts.

Praise ye him, sun and moon: praise him,
all ye stars of light.

Praise him, ye heavens of heavens and ye
waters that be above the heavens.

Let them praise the name of the Lord: for
he commanded and they were created.

He hath also established them for ever and
ever: he hath made a decree which shall not
pass. (Psalm 148:1–6, KJV)

A Declaration of Love

In the midst of this heaven-filling sound, God declared: "And I will dwell among these people, and they will be my people and I will be their God! And I will love them and they will love Me. And they will worship me!"

Under the leadership of Lucifer's voice, the praise and awe of God among the angels was overwhelming! I thought of the psalm:

When I consider thy heavens, the work of
thy fingers, the moon and the stars, which thou
hast ordained; what is man, that thou art mindful
of him? and the son of man that thou dost visit
him? For thou hast made him a little lower than
the angels, and hast crowned him with glory and
beauty. Thou hast made him to have dominion over
the works of thy hands; thou hast put all things
under his feet. (Psalm 8:3–6, JUB)

The Ultimate Declaration,
and an Unlawful Imagination

And then I heard God declare, "And I am going to set a Son of Man—one of them—to be King over the heavens and the earth—over all creation!"

Suddenly, with the declaration that a Man would be placed over

God's creation, I saw a slight change in Lucifer's countenance. Michael also saw the change, but none of the other angels appeared to be aware of it. God did not reveal the identity of the Son of Man who would rule creation. He had finished. With that, the impenetrable curtains closed.

Much as after a stadium event on earth, the shouting gradually died away and the angels went back to their places. Yet awe still consumed them because of what God had decreed, and because of the sheer experience for most of them, who were hearing the voice of God for the first time.

(Note: When the curtains of light were open during God's declarations, they were not sufficiently open to see "Him who dwells in unapproachable light." A measure of His light did, however, shine through the opening.)

 The End of Vision Five

FURTHER COMMENTARY:
WHAT'S THE POINT?

At this point I want to clarify the point. The visions are about to take us into the great mystery of our six-day creation, the human race, and good and evil. Why is it important to know that creation began in heaven, before time? The answer was given through the prophet Isaiah, who wrote: "I am God, and there is none like me, declaring the end from the beginning, and from ancient times things not yet done, My counsel shall stand, and I will accomplish all my purpose" (Isaiah 46:9–10, ESV).

If God decrees the end from the beginning, and we situate the "beginning" in the wrong place, we will misread His purposes—and shift His entire timeline. The point is: God requires precision. He is not slack in His strategies; His plans require dedicated attention. If you opened a book, or walked into a movie halfway through, how much of the story would you really understand? This I know, God has chosen this time in history to unveil events that occurred *Before the Beginning.*

Second, since "all Scripture is God-breathed" (2 Timothy 3:16, CJB), everything recorded in Scripture is important for understanding the bigger picture of life. The Bible is not a pick-and-choose compilation of sixty-six books of human origin. It explains the context in which all creation exists, beginning with the Creator, God.

Life Did Not Begin in the Garden of Eden

Since I was invited to observe this series of visions, and have weighed these visions against Scripture, it has become clear that God and the creation of His kingdom predate the natural world. Before anything existed, there was God. "In the beginning God . . ."

(Genesis 1:1)

Why did God give me visions of what happened before the creation of the natural world? Perhaps Isaiah gives us a clue: "Remember this, and show yourselves men; recall to mind, O you transgressors" (Isaiah 46:5, NKJV). Sin has clouded mankind's vision of spiritual realities. We need reminding. These visions were given to remind all people everywhere, that there is a God to whom each of us must give account. Who, besides Creator God, has made a universe, explained why He has created it, why things happen as they do, and how it will all turn out?

Creation is the medium through which God chose to reveal himself to men and angels. The heavens do in fact, "declare the glory of God and the firmament [space] shows his handiwork. Day unto day utters speech and night unto night reveals knowledge. There is no speech nor language where their voice is not heard" (Psalm 19:1, NKJV). All creation is responsible to know its Creator. Everything began with God. Eden was only one part of God's handiwork, but it was a great part and perhaps closest to His heart. Eden was a garden within the garden of Creation, yet, life did not begin there.

The Context of Creation

The context of creation must go back to God, or else everything else will be thrown off track. Beginning at its highest point of created space, God's first priority was to establish His kingdom. Mankind would follow.

God's design for creation was neither secular nor religious. Everything was created by Jesus for the glory of the Father. For a complete and exact pattern of what the heavenly temple looks like, we have only to refer back to the tabernacle in the wilderness: "And let them [Israel] make Me a sanctuary, that I may dwell among them. According to all that I show you, that is, the pattern of the tabernacle and the pattern of all its furnishings, just so shall you make it" (Exodus 25:8–9, NKJV). From earth, Moses received the entire pattern of the temple in heaven. It was the most extensive revelation ever given to a single human being. Moses took fifty chapters to explain the tabernacle and its ministries. God himself said only Moses spoke to Him face to face. Yet this did not mean to imply that Moses actually went into the Holy Place and saw the full extent of the Burning Flame of light, as one sees another human being. It did mean He encountered God on a level beyond any other mortal.

In whatever way God chooses to reveal himself, it always has some degree of hidden mystery. When a mystery of God's plan is unveiled it always has an impact of eternal importance.

Human beings have always tried to separate the two worlds of the spiritual and natural, but they belong together. We live in a world that is both spiritual and natural. It is a world that was created for eternity.

What's the point? We live in a world of great struggle and great destiny, and God expects us to mature in spiritual understanding. Jesus said, "Hypocrites! You can discern the face of the sky but you cannot discern the signs of the times [you lack understanding of what is going on in the world around you]" (Matthew 16:3, NKJV).

My visions put things in context. They state the utter reality and sovereignty of God: His total power, His flawless precision, His unbeatable strategies, which, without one exception, always have the last say. In Greek, one of His names is *Pantokrator*—the All in All! Keep fixed on this reality and the next vision I received will open worlds of understanding.

Vision Six
LUCIFER AND
THE COMING CREATION

BEFORE God's declaration of a New Universe (our six-day Creation), the camaraderie of the three archangels was flawless. Discord was not a consideration. They were highest in rank, revelation, intelligence, and ability, although they continued to seek understanding of spiritual things.

(The Apostle Peter wrote that godly understanding has come to mankind by the Holy Spirit, through the Hebrew prophets, to the apostles who taught it to the early church, and finally as the church goes out and shares the Good News.) The angels continue to desire this treasure:

> To them [the prophets] it was revealed that,
> not to themselves, but to us they were ministering
> the things which now have been reported to
> you through those who have preached the gospel
> to you by the Holy Spirit sent from heaven—
> things which angels desire to look into.
> (1 Peter 1:12, NKJV)

Following the announcement of the New Creation, I saw Lucifer alone, pacing and pensive, with a look of deep thought on his face. In a way that I cannot explain, I was thinking his thoughts and knew what he was thinking. I understood that Lucifer had a much greater revelation of what God had declared than did the hosts of angels. The common angels did not appear to have perceived any of the ramifications of God's decree on their lives or on the heavenly realm. I do not know to what degree Michael and Gabriel had understanding. I only know they left the announcement rejoicing. As yet, Lucifer had not rebelled.

Lucifer Reasoned

We have noted that Lucifer was a glorious and powerful archangel. When rejoicing broke out at God's declaration, I heard Lucifer's voice above those of all of the innumerable angels. His deep voice sounded like a mega-sound system, and its roar drew every other voice into his anointing. Even the stones on his robe shot out glorious beams of light at the sound of his praise. Among the created beings, in appearance there was no angel with the glory of Lucifer. God had announced him, "perfect in his ways until iniquity was found in him" (see Ezekiel 12:15). Yet, even in his superiority to all other angels, Lucifer did not see the bigger plan.

Things Can Be Lost

As I was watching Lucifer, it became clear to me that in God's system, *things, positions,* and even *eternity* can be forfeited. Human theology cannot paint the full picture, neither the determinism that says your circumstances dictate your destiny, nor the predestination that says everything will turn out as it should. While God's ultimate plans cannot be thwarted, mankind and many of God's desires for man are truly at risk. God has hidden His plans from men and angels, only allowing them to manifest at specific times, according to His wisdom.

While believers are commissioned to go out and "make disciples of all nations" (see Matthew 28:19), they are also warned not to "cast their pearls before swine" (see Matthew 7:6). Careless handling of sacred things can be costly, if not fatal. When God healed King Hezekiah of a fatal illness, his enemy, the king of Babylon, sent some of his men with letters and a gift to congratulate the King. In an act of naïve hospitality, Hezekiah did a foolish thing and showed his enemies all of his extensive treasures. Then God sent the prophet Isaiah to Hezekiah with this word: "Hear the word of the Lord. Behold the days come, that all that is in thy house, and that which thy fathers have laid up in store to this day, shall be carried into Babylon: nothing shall be left, saith the Lord" (2 Kings 20:17, KJV).

The Birth of Sin

I saw Lucifer walking back and forth in an area alone, in deep contemplation about the New Creation. I came to understand that, as an archangel, Lucifer had greater revelation than ordinary angels about the ramifications of God's declarations. At the same time, I also realized the limitations of Lucifer's understanding of these new creations, human beings. It was then I understood that revelation from God is given, not developed through reasoning.

What I heard Lucifer reasoning deserves every person's closest attention. Sin was conceived in the heart of Lucifer:

"This is unique; there have never been such beings. Human beings are going to be created in the image and likeness of God."

"Created in His image, these new beings will be able to love and worship God with an unparalleled capacity."

"I wonder what their worship is going to be like?"

"Oh, to be the object of their worship!"

"What glorious beings!"

Then came the fatal question:

"But why would God appoint one of them king over this new creation? . . . even over heaven!"

"Why one of them and not Me?" (Lucifer did not know the true identity of the Son of Man who would be appointed King.)

"I know that what has been decreed is irreversible, but . . . ?"

And the dread strategy:

"For these human beings to truly love God, it will involve choice—the choice to love Him. But they could also choose not to love him—or even choose to worship another."

 The End of Vision Six

FURTHER COMMENTARY:
THE GARDEN OF CHOICE

Have you ever wondered why God gave Lucifer freedom of choice? Or why He has given the human race free will? In the name of reason, why didn't God just destroy Lucifer? And if He is really all-powerful, why doesn't He just cure all of the world's ills?

Certainly, before creation, the risk of choice was known to God. In wisdom, God considered both the risk (the loss of people), and the cost (the death of His Son, "the Lamb slain from before the foundations"), and He remained true to His own righteous nature. To answer the questions of "Why?" the only logical conclusion could be that, above all else, covenant faithfulness had to be *real*. Choice is the one dynamic that makes love, worship, and covenant faithfulness authentic.

In every circumstance, God demands the "real thing." The Ten Commandments given to Moses confirm God's commitment to the righteous character. In the series of visions I was privileged to observe, I came to realize that every soul counts to God, not because of what any person "brings to the plate," but because of what every son of Adam, having a legitimate, blood-bought opportunity, can become. To have *people, in His own image and likeness,* is God's ultimate desire.

Authenticity, the Test in the Garden

From *eretz* (the land) God formed a man and breathed into him the breath of life. "And man became a living soul" (Genesis 2:7, KJV). He then took a rib from Adam's side and made a partner for him, called woman, and Eve became the mother of all living.

Why did God take a rib from Adam's side to create woman? Why not make her from the soil as well? Because Eve from the soil was not a part of Adam in the way she would be if she came from his own body. In coming from Adam, Eve was of the same *substance*. With his love deposited into her heart, and her love deposited into his heart, the man and woman were authentically one and in a covenant relationship with each other. As Eve was of the body of the First Adam so the covenant people are of the body of the Last Adam—Christ.

Adam and Eve were God's prototype of the covenant He seeks to have with His people.. Paul called this, *the mystery of the church:* "For this reason a man will leave his father and mother and be united to his wife, and the two will become one flesh [quoted from Genesis 2:24]. This is a profound mystery—but I am talking about Christ and the church" (Ephesians 5: 31–32, NIV).

This bond of unity was what Lucifer most desired. No angel had a blood/family relationship with God. Only man was made in God's image and likeness (meaning as near to God as possible without being God, only slightly different; God is eternal, mankind is created). This oneness with God was the reason Lucifer/Satan showed up in the garden looking to take the object of God's desire for himself. Employing the aid of the clever serpent, Lucifer managed to engage Eve in conversation with fallen logic, and Eve lost! "You will not surely die!" the serpent whispered. "In the day you eat of it your eyes will be opened, and you will be like God, knowing good and evil" (Genesis 3:4–5, NKJV).

Freedom of choice is a reality. Standing on the brink of life and death, Eve demonstrated that reality by making the decision to risk

God's warning in her pursuit of that impassioned urge to learn more about the forbidden.

No surprise to God—Eve fell. Adam fell. The entire human race in every generation since has fallen for the same deception. But in His foreknowledge, God is light years ahead of every step fallen creation takes. In the garden, more of God's mystery was unveiled. For its role in the fall, forever the clever serpent would now crawl on the ground, "for its food will be dust" (Isaiah 65:25, CJB). And Satan received a declaration that sent him smarting all the way back to his dingy kingdom realm: "And I will put enmity between you and the woman, and between your offspring and hers; He will crush your head, and you will strike his heel" (Genesis 3:15, NIV).

God's Man-Ruler was on the way! What a blow! God would now expose Satan to the entire human race. Those who chose his deception would lose their souls and identity forever, but through the work of His Spirit, those who chose God would find life and light.

The Planet at War

One of the oldest examples of this war on Earth is told in the ancient story of Job. A few hundred years after the Fall, a famous man who lived in Uz caught Satan's eye. He went to God and made a bid for Job's soul. God gave Satan latitude to afflict Job, but he could not take his life. During Job's terrible but revealing trial, he remained faithful to God, but he did pose the number one question of all time: "*Why?*" Finally, God decided to end the trial. He began to answer man's question with an interrogation of Job, posing 184 questions, such as the following:

> Who is this, darkening my plans with his
> ignorant words? Stand up like a man, and brace
> yourself; I will ask questions; and you, give the
> answers!
> Where were you when I laid the foundations of
> the earth? Tell me if you know so much.

Do you know who determined its dimensions,
or who stretched the measuring line across it?

On what were its bases sunk, or who laid its
cornerstone, when the morning stars sang together,
and all the Sons of God shouted for joy? . . .

Have you gone down to the springs of the sea
or explored the limits of the deep? Have the gates
of death been revealed to you, the gates of death-
like darkness? Have you surveyed the full extent
of the earth? Say so if you know it all! (Job 38:2–7,
16–18, CJB)

Just as God had pierced the darkness, filled the dome with celestial lights and created Earth by His Holy Spirit, He would penetrate the invisible spiritual darkness that now moved stealthily across His choice planet.

And whereas God spoke directly to the first man and woman whom He had made in His image, after the Fall He would speak mainly through human channels known as prophets. But because God is a strategist and the earth was now a battleground, God's plans revealed through His prophets would be revealed in partially veiled language, and they would be called mysteries and hidden things.

The prophets themselves only understood the things they spoke in part; their duty was to pull back the curtain on the plan of God from age to age through "types" and "shadows." We might think of the prophets as inspired "narrators" for the Author. Through God-breathed words they unveiled the plans, scene by scene. Moses was the prophet who wrote the first earth scene in the Book of Genesis.

Vision Seven
THE ARM OF THE LORD

I N Vision Seven, I was to see something I will never forget, something I consider foundational to biblical faith. This vision was a series of four scenes.

At this point there had never been any disharmony among the three archangels—no disharmony in the heavens, period.

The First Scene

The first scene was that of Michael, Gabriel, and Lucifer after the announcement about the New Creation. Michael had seen Lucifer's slight change of countenance on the day of the announcement, but had said nothing. The three angels were talking. Each of the archangels had a stone in the location of the human heart that glowed with the same light in which God clothed himself. That light appeared to be a part of the archangels. During their conversation, Lucifer's stone wavered faintly in intensity; the others noticed it, but neither acknowledged what they had just seen. Lucifer then tried discreetly to move his strap over his dimming light, to hide the wavering glow.

Later, when they were alone, Michael and Gabriel said to one another, "did you see that?" Both were concerned.

Then Michael and Gabriel were called into the presence of God. Lucifer was not there. This is what I understood:

> Michael said to God, "Lord we saw something that disturbed us."

The Lord responded, "I know! Do not say anything about this!"

Both Michael and Gabriel knew something was not right, but they did not understand the magnitude of what was happening

The Second Scene

In the second scene, Michael and Gabriel received reports from their captains of mild strife between some angels under their command and Lucifer's. Strife in heaven was unheard-of. The three archangels continued to interact. By this time, both Michael and Gabriel were aware of the growing change in Lucifer. The change had become more evident through the increased dimming of the light that glowed within each of the three angels. Neither Michael nor Gabriel communicated anything to their captains concerning what they had seen in Lucifer.

The Third Scene

Troubled by what they had seen and now heard, Michael and Gabriel requested an audience with God. They were again called into the presence of God. From the events that happened in this meeting with God, it became clear to me that even the archangels did not know all that *has since* been revealed to believers through God's Word.

Michael was addressing God and recounting to Him the strong concern he had about Lucifer's change and the alien strife that was reported among the angels. Michael continued with his statement, expressing with great concern, "Lord You have to do something!"

But before another word could come out of his mouth, the *arm of the Lord* shot out from within the fire (yet as a part of the fire), and it literally blew the two archangels off their feet, sending them sailing backward, where they landed on the floor. Their flight was accompanied by the booming voice of God: "HOLD YOUR PEACE!" Then the Lord proceeded to instruct them, concluding with "say nothing" [of what they had reported concerning Lucifer].

Michael and Gabriel were stunned by what they had just seen.

Until they were dismissed they stayed glued to the floor looking straight up into the atmosphere, listening to God's instruction. Watching this scene, I had the immediate understanding that this was the first time they had ever seen the "arm of the Lord."

The Fourth Scene

Once again, I was back in the conference room, where the archangels' captains were seated at the round table awaiting them. Their backs were to the doors where Michael and Gabriel would enter. Although I never saw the doors open, both archangels were suddenly inside the conference room.

Michael was to my left looking toward Gabriel, who was to my right and looking toward Michael. They both were looking as though they had seen the most astounding thing in all the heavens (and they had)! Michael began to speak in a powerful tongue (language) to Gabriel, and Gabriel spoke back in that language just as powerfully. The tone of their voices turned the attention of the captains toward them, with a look of concern. They sensed something had happened.

Back and forth, the archangels kept speaking intently. (God supernaturally allowed me to understand what was being said.) Then one of Michael's captains spoke up, "Michael! What happened? What is it?"

Michael turned to him, and in that same forcefully intense language he began to speak to him. The captain responded "Michael! Michael! I don't understand archangel language!"

Michael then told them in their language, *"God has an arm!"* At these words, his captain responded with strong emotion, "Michael! What are you saying! We all know The Great Creator is invisible, and He dwells in unapproachable light! What are you saying?"

Michael then turned to Gabriel and responded to his captain: *"The Invisible God has an arm! He revealed His arm to us!"* Gabriel affirmed what Michael had said, that they had both seen the Arm of the Lord!

Though none of them understood this revelation to the extent that it would be revealed in time, yet they remained in awe of the Arm of the Lord. The archangels remanded their captains to silence about what they had just been told.

 The End of Vision Seven

FURTHER COMMENTARY:
THE LANGUAGE OF ANGELS

This vision had transformational impact on my understanding, as it has had on others with whom I have shared these divine encounters. My understanding of Paul's statement in 1 Corinthians 13:1, was confirmed: "Though I speak in the tongues of men and angels," was not a figure of speech. Angels are multilingual in heaven's languages as well as earth's international language pool!

What mankind calls "New Technology," is only a small portion of the communication abilities of the Creator. All angelic and human wisdom combined are a "drop in the bucket." I also understood once again that angels had no revelation of what we call the Trinity. They had only heard but never seen the Word of God. In hearing Him, they never fathomed the possibility of the Word of God coming out of the Unapproachable Light in bodily form.

When the Arm of the Lord manifested, it literally came out of the Light, as a part of the Light. The Arm literally formed from the substance of the Presence as it projected itself out. The Light became Arm as it pushed forward, and then became Light again as it returned. Standing there gazing up at the sky, I knew as I had never known before that Jesus is the Man-Ruler who is of the Father; He came out *from the Father,* and He is *one with the Father.* There is one God, the Savior of fallen mankind. No religious leader qualifies even to stand rank or ever be compared with the Arm of the Lord.

The Apostle John wrote of the Arm of the Lord, saying:

> But although he had done so many signs before
> them, yet they did not believe in him, that the word
> of Isaiah the prophet might be fulfilled, which he
> spoke, Lord, who shall believe our report? and to
> whom has *the arm of the Lord* been revealed?
> (John 12:37–38, JUB, emphasis added)

The *arm of the Lord* is Yeshua–Jesus–the Word of God in
human form.

The Misinformation of "Religious Thought"

Just as all people breathe air, all people breathe worship. Air is
essential to life, no one rejects it even when it comes through a tube. All
souls breathe worship, even when they are misinformed. Conflicting
religions and religious thought result from lack of truth.

Jesus said "I AM . . . the Truth" (John 14:6, CJB). Read it this way:
He said, "I AM (The one who spoke with Moses) . . . the Truth." The
"I AM" of the Hebrew Scriptures, is the "I AM" of the New Testament.
One Book, One God, One Manifestation of God in human form who
is the saving Arm by which confused humanity may find life.

Vision Eight
THE EARTH, THE REVOLT, THE WORD
In the beginning God created the heavens and the earth. (Genesis 1:1)

I N this final vision there were two scenes: first there was the creation of the earth, and second there was Lucifer's public declaration of his intentions, God's response to Lucifer, and the Word of God revealed in full bodily form.

As we have discovered so far, one of the primary elements of the visions I saw was the revelation of a definite unfolding of events in the heavens *before the earth was created.* It is impossible to measure the amount of time that passed between the creation of the heavens and the creation of earth, because these were events that were before time began. Paul wrote, ". . . according to His own purpose and grace which was given to us in Christ Jesus *before time began*" (2 Timothy 1:8, NKJV, emphasis added).

It was my understanding that the order of events matters. Iniquity entered into God's creation in the heart of Lucifer at some point between the announcement of the Man King, and the beginning of our six-day creation. After iniquity entered Lucifer, darkness progressively spread into creation. But as yet there had been no public rebellion.

God Creates the Earth
Genesis 1:2 says, "The earth was without form and void and darkness was upon the face of the deep. And the Spirit of God moved

upon the face of the waters." In Hebrew, "without form and void" is *tohu va bohu,* translated "waste and empty." Many people believe that God created the earth good, and by the rebellion of Lucifer the earth then became waste and empty. But is this accurate?

I contacted Hebrew scholar, Dr. Walt Kaiser, and asked him the following: "Does the text of Genesis 1:2 grammatically support the idea that God created good and then it "became" *tohu va bohu* (or dark and void)?" He said the text does not support this. He went on to explain that there is a very definite way in Hebrew to say "it became," and that this is not it.

So why this little Hebrew lesson? Because God had given me understanding from the vision that the earth was in darkness when He created it. It was the darkness that resulted from the iniquity of Lucifer. In other words, *Luciferian darkness predates the creation of the earth.*

On the first day, when the earth was created, God laid its foundations in darkness. I did not see the process of creation. But Scripture tells us how it unfolded. His initial thrust was to penetrate the darkness with His word:

> Then God said, "Let there be light"; and there was light. And God saw the light, that it was good; and God divided the light from the darkness. God called the light Day, and the darkness He called Night. So the evening and the morning were the first day. (Gen. 1:3-5, NKJV)

This should inspire even the smallest faith. John spoke to this moment when he said, "The light shines in the darkness, and the darkness has not overcome it" (John 1:5, ESV). Just the fact that no amount of darkness can overcome the smallest amount of light assures us that God has always had the victory! But the question remains, why did God not do away with Lucifer before our creation, so that all would be peace?

The answer to that question is this: There was divine purpose in God allowing the rebellion to run its course in the heavens and then spread darkness into our creation. There was purpose in God creating in darkness. There was purpose in God allowing the fallen archangel the freedom to rebel. There was purpose in God using six days to create our earth rather than one magical moment. I now understood that God's design made it necessary for creation to begin in *seed form*, in order for His plans and purposes to develop. "The kingdom of heaven is as a seed."

Scene One: It was only after God penetrated the darkness and created the earth that Lucifer advanced with his entire host to the base of heavenly Mount Zion and declared his intentions. This set up the scene for the breach.

Scene Two: Lucifer and his four captains were mounted on horses, as well other angels of lesser rank, along with a host of foot soldiers, as they came marching in rank and file to the base of the Mountain of God. The angels who had not chosen to ally themselves with the rebellion looked on with consternation. There was a hush throughout the heavenly host.

Positioned at the foot of the mountain before the throne, Lucifer then declared his intention to depose the Man-King God would appoint over His new creation. Lucifer declared boldly, "I will become the king of this creation! I will become the object of worship of those made in the image of God! I am the one worthy to be like the Most High over his people!"

Then the veils of light around the Most High began to draw back. The Fire of God became visible from the front for the first time before the host. This was staggering to all who had never seen the presence of the Lord! The mountain began to rumble and the heavens began to tremble. The Word of God was heard by all existence. Isaiah and Ezekiel record the exact wording:

> How you are fallen from heaven,
> O Lucifer, son of the morning! (Isaiah 14:12, NKJV)
> You were the seal of perfection,

Full of wisdom and perfect in beauty. . . .
You were the anointed cherub who covers!
(Ezekiel 28:12–14, NKJV)

Right in the midst of this declaration, the Word of God began to become visible, just as the Arm of the Lord had been revealed. The Word of God began taking bodily form simultaneous to being heard. Once His body was fully formed, the declaration, never pausing, continued, but it was now coming from Him. The voice went from being omnipresent to proceeding from God in bodily form—with power that shook the heavens. It was clear that the voice continuing was the Word of God:

I established you; [Note: the Word created Lucifer.]
You were on the holy mountain of God;
You walked back and forth in the midst of
fiery stones.
You were perfect in your ways from the day
you were created,
Till iniquity was found in you. . . .
Your heart was lifted up because of
your beauty;
You corrupted your wisdom for the sake of
your splendor. (Ezekiel 28:14–15, 17, NKJV)
For you have said in your heart: ". . . I will be
like the Most High." Yet you shall be brought down
to Sheol, to the lowest depths of the Pit.
(Isaiah 14:13, 15, NKJV)
You have become a horror,
And shall be no more forever.
(Ezekiel 28:14, NKJV)

From the blast of God's voice, Lucifer's captains were catapulted from their horses, blown backward through the air, and then disappeared. As the declaration continued, the horses, along with the foot soldiers, were all catapulted in like manner and disappeared. "By the blast of God they perish, And by the breath of His anger they are consumed" (Job 4:9, NKJV). Lucifer was alone on his horse when I heard the Word conclude, "Go and do what you will!" At this, Lucifer turned to ride out in the same direction from which he had come.

Michael, Gabriel, and the rest of the angels stood, transfixed. They had watched and heard the unimaginable! They had seen the Word of God! They had seen God in bodily form! It had never entered into the mind of the angels that God would take bodily form! Upon seeing this manifestation, they erupted into a celebration of praise and awe.

Things I Understood Concerning Lucifer

Lucifer never envisioned or plotted to go into the Holy Place of the invisible, omniscient, omnipotent Creator and dethrone Him. Lucifer had set His sights on God's glorious plan, on the human beings created in His image. He understood, to some degree, what it meant to have beings in the likeness of God. This meant they would be the closest possible image to God, without being God. *Lucifer desired to be the god of this world.*

Moreover, Lucifer had never seen the Lord in bodily form. Though he had great understanding and power, he did not know the mysteries yet to be unveiled. Lucifer did not know, when he declared his intentions, that he had set himself in direct conflict with the Word of God, who had just appeared and proclaimed his end. Lucifer did not know that this Son of God would one day enter into Earth's creation story, coming in flesh as the Son of Man, to face and defeat the Resister himself. In God's great story of love and rescue, Lucifer was brilliant, but he did not know the depth of desire or matchless power and wisdom of the true Sovereign.

This is the end of Vision Eight, but it was just the beginning of an explosion of scriptural unveilings.

The Book of Genesis is the first book God inspired Moses to write.

That is because the Book of Genesis (Beginnings) is foundational to the mysteries of the kingdom that were to be revealed.

The End of Vision Eight

FURTHER COMMENTARY:
GOD'S NEW CREATION

This is the end of direct commentary on the eight visions, which were just the beginning of an explosion of scriptural understanding for me. The Book of Genesis is the first book in the Bible because this book is foundational to the mysteries of the kingdom that are waiting to be discovered. Since my brief visionary view of God before our world was created, Genesis has been the springboard to the hidden mysteries given throughout the Bible.

In the remaining chapters of this book, I will share some of the insights that continue to unfold as I study and teach the Word of God. I hope that this understanding will serve to enlighten and enrich a generation trapped by increasing spiritual confusion.

The Bible refers to the unfolding of God's plan as "mysteries," (Greek, *musterion*), which explain life, its purpose and ultimate destiny. Knowledge of God comes not by force, but by desire and spiritual revelation. He strategically guides His people through their veiled understanding of events, past their clever Adversary, until they have reached the light.

Creation was conceived in the mind and heart of the Holy God. It began in the highest heavens, but it will conclude here on planet Earth. Eternity is on the horizon and the battle for truth is increasing, but the Eternal God has already declared and proven himself sovereign. The visions I received are like an embossed invitation to intently reexamine the Word of God. I also consider them a wake-up call to stand with the Truth in the face of great ideological and spiritual opposition.

VISION EIGHT

On the following pages we will explore further what these messages mean for our lives today and in light of eternity, according to the Scriptures.

SECTION TWO

Chapter One
THE KINGDOM OF GOD

WHAT do we mean by the term "Kingdom of God"?
There is an infinite domain that is solely God. From eternity, God exists both outside His creation and within it. The Kingdom of God is the domain of God from within His creation. God chose to establish a domain within His creation in which He could enter into His plans and interact with mankind. Yet, He is never limited to His creation.

All world religions that believe in a deity visualize their god or gods as unknowable, because they do not have "eyes to see and ears to hear," that is, Holy Spirit enlightenment. Jesus said, "When the spirit of truth comes, he will guide you into all the truth" (John 16:13, CJB).

Whether information is natural or spiritual, the interpretation of information has one of two sources: truth or lie. This is why one of God's first warnings to Israel was against idol worship. False images of people, things, careers, ideologies, and philosophies distort truth and cause whole generations to build their entire culture around false gods, through which Lucifer's kingdom works.

Revolutions, past and present, come from the kingdom of darkness in pursuit of the kingdom of light. Lucifer's hunger for power, working through human nature hungry for power, is the root of all oppressive revolution.

The Results Are In

The results are in, and proof of Lucifer's failures are as old as human history. Instead of proving that his dark kingdom is what mankind really needs, his world system screams with human misery. If Lucifer's dark kingdom is stronger than God's kingdom, then why is the earth littered with monuments to his crumbled empires? Instead of being the one who establishes the nations in peace, he is the model of the "one who did weaken the nations" (Isaiah 14:12, KJV).

Results expose the source. The earth is in conflict because two-thirds of the world is enslaved in a spiritually dark information-glut. How much Satan understands is debatable, but he does know that God's kingdom purpose is slated to "cover the earth as the waters cover the sea," and his strategy is to drive back this flood with his own dark waters of information.

Change Your Mind

When Jesus [whose name means, "God Saves"], was born as "King of the Jews," His ministry began with these words, "Repent, for the *kingdom of heaven* is at hand" (Matthew 3:2, NKJV, emphasis added). When the disciples asked Jesus to teach them to pray, He said: "Our Father which art in heaven, hallowed by thy name; Thy *kingdom come;* Thy will [kingdom authority] be done on earth as it is in heaven" (Matthew 6:10, KJV, emphasis added). Jesus also added this command: "Seek ye first the *kingdom of God,* and his righteousness, and all these [natural] things shall be added unto you" (Matthew 6:33, KJV, emphasis added).

The source from which all thought is weighed is God and His system of information. And before the earth's formulations, measurements, and foundation were fastened to a cornerstone, the kingdom system was already set in place.

Christians often use the word Gospel to describe their message. But what does that mean? Does it only say that a good man named Jesus died for sin? It's more than that. The gospel is, "The good news of the *kingdom*" (Matthew 9:35, NIV, emphasis added.) The good news of the kingdom is the King! In the face of the certain death of civilization, the Creator himself has intervened and is offering a way of rescue!

During His earthly tenure, and with only a partial record of all He spoke, Jesus referred to His kingdom 139 times. According to Him, Abraham, Isaac, and Jacob are already in that kingdom, and will one day be celebrating the Feast of Tabernacles, (Sukkot) in Jerusalem with the saints! "Moreover, I tell you that many will come from the east and from the west to take their place at the feast in the Kingdom of Heaven with Avrahim, Yitz/chak and Ya'akov [Abraham, Isaac, Jacob]" (Matthew 8:11, CJB).

On the surface, Jesus' parables seem little more than good stories told by a good man. But the parables He told were revelations of the coming kingdom that will clean up and dominate, or eliminate, all world-system governments. Jesus said, "I will open my mouth in parables and I will utter things kept secret *from the foundation of the world*" (Matthew 13:34–35, JUB, emphasis added).

Jesus' stories were interesting and made good moral points, but they were told for a reason far beyond that. The kingdom parables were told in order to reveal the reality and nature of the Kingdom of Heaven. Because "all have sinned and come short of the glory of God" (see Romans 3:23), the kingdom remains a mystery to much of the world's population at any given time. Yet the glories of the kingdom are available to them. ("Glory" in Hebrew is *kabod,* from the root *kabed,* which means "numerous, rich, honorable.")

The opposite of *kabed* is "burdensome, severe, and dull." In other words, when humanity rejects God and the spiritual benefits of His kingdom, life becomes burdensome, harsh, and dull. A nation and a world in rebellion to God carry heavy burdens; life is often cruel and severe. Boredom with the things of this world chases us at every turn, causing us to make devastating choices.

Before one atom of matter came into existence, before there was a DNA chain of life to be examined, God decreed a plan for life. It was not a religion, it was not a philosophy, it was not a theology, it was God and His kingdom on earth. Ministers, orators, and writers refer to the parables of Jesus as if they are quoting some socially-conscious sage or one of many religious leaders. It never occurs to them that they are handling a kingdom mystery ordained by the Creator before the world began.

What Is the Kingdom of Heaven Like?

To this generation, the kingdom is largely irrelevant and virtually invisible. The Ten Commandments and the image of Christ are being pulled from walls and deleted from textbooks. The Bible, the best documented ancient text in existence, is intellectually snubbed and ignored as inferior to the bits and pieces of other ancient documents. The Bible is more than history, but it is the best document of history man possesses. By design, the kingdom is like a small seed, but one word planted by God gives birth to a library of wisdom and knowledge. One note enters the ear and a symphony fills the hall! With God, small can be enormous!

Jesus told them a parable about the Kingdom of Heaven, which he compared to the leaven that a woman mixes with flour (see Luke 13:20–21). Life without the Spirit is like tasteless flour, it gives no satisfaction and it flies away with the wind. The kingdom of heaven leavens life. It gives rise to purpose and meaning and taste, even to the smallest moments.

The Kingdom of Heaven is small in the eyes of those who are caught up in the overrated present world system, the power structures of the darkness of this age. It is foolishness to those who worship the intellect or the passions of the senses. It is fantasy to those who deny the sermons of nature, who love the praise of men more than the praise that comes from God.

Even for those who believe, the "cares of life" make it hardly worth setting aside time every day to study, pray, and pursue God. Many do postural meditation for the sake of their bodies and fitness, but they fail to discipline their ear to hear the voice of the Spirit, Who has been sent to guide us into all truth. Fitness brings a measure of physical improvement, and better quality of health, but without exception it is only temporary.

Evidence of the eternal kingdom is all around us, but different interpretations of what is going on consume the media, often with reports of disastrous results. As in Noah's day, the majority will not understand until the flood comes and washes them all away. But there is also a warning to those with eyes to see and ears to hear: Jesus said, "He who has an ear let him hear what the Spirit says to the churches" (Revelation 2:29, NKJV). It is possible for seeing eyes to grow dim and for hearing ears to grow dull, for people to ignore what is going on in the world and to remain willfully ignorant of the great battle between the two great kingdoms of darkness and light.

The Powers That Be

The counsels of man are, at best, flawed and God takes no counsel from man. Why then should we call men the "authorities," and run only to them in our weak moments? Nothing compares to one word from God.

To know that you are a part of an eternal plan that began *before creation* is living knowledge that will continue to impart life in the barren desert. Creator God put ages of forethought into the universe before He made it. Man cannot even hope to master the powers that exist on this earth. Floods overrun our best dams; tornados pick up our buildings and scatter them like straw; droughts starve us; tsunamis stir the waters and thousands disappear. The earth is the Lord's, and all the powers it possesses belong to Him. Both His natural and spiritual kingdoms are unstoppable as well as flawless. Human systems are no match to God's.

Furthermore, the powers that be are about to change hands: "And the seventh angel sounded; and there were great voices in heaven, saying, The kingdoms of this world are become the kingdoms of our Lord, and of his Christ; and he shall reign for ever and ever" (Revelation 11:15, KJV).

Chapter Two
THE HEART OF GOD

WHAT did the visions reveal about the heart (desires) of God? The heart of God is expressed through His plans; His heart, desires, and plans are interchangeable. God's heart is pure. He says only what He means, and He means exactly what He says. His counselor is His own wisdom. He cannot be deceived, nor can be persuaded to act other than by His own superior intelligence.

In the first vision I saw a glowing city where everything—every angel, every building, every object—reflected the Shekinah glory of God. Like a well-cut diamond, everything animate and inanimate had been created to reflect His glory. It was a picture of the future of creation when His image, His heart, His holy desires will cover all creation "as the waters cover the sea."

Imagine everything on earth, including the earth itself, glowing like the stars. "Ugly" would be a thing of the past. Aging lines on the face and soul would be forgotten. Everything would be eternally beautiful. Every person would be a portrait of wisdom and creative imagination. God's desire is that the curse presently on all creation be washed away by His glory until every spot and wrinkle are washed away by the infusion of eternal light.

The Capital City

To fill up His heart's desire, God began by establishing a kingdom with a capital city, New Jerusalem. As Sovereign of all intelligences, He positioned His throne in the center of this city. In the view of

His throne, all city-dwellers have the comfort of His Presence. His protection is certain, His own enjoyment as an integral part of life is without question. To govern and protect His kingdom, God created angels for the task of assisting Him in carrying out His plans.

On earth, God established a corresponding city to New Jerusalem; it was established on a piece of land that would eventually be called Israel. Beleaguered little earthly Jerusalem is a far cry from the glory reflected in the heavenly city. Yet, after centuries of attacks against its existence, the unconquerable plan of God for both cities continues to survive.

It was in dusty little Jerusalem on the Day of Pentecost that the Holy Spirit brought the New Covenant promised in Jeremiah:

> Behold the days are coming says the Lord,
> when I will make a new covenant with the house
> of Israel. . . . [T]he city [Jerusalem] shall be
> built. . . . It shall not be plucked up or thrown down
> any more forever. (Jeremiah 31:31, 38, 40, NKJV)

God works in expansive terms of eternity. His desires do not diminish with time, nor does He tire of His plans for His people. At the outpouring of His Holy Spirit, God entered into humanity, both Jew and Gentile, with the plan to eventually meld all creation into one sacred universe and all humanity into "one new man." We might say that the Kingdom of God was the Creator's inter-galactic plan for a creation-wide harvest of those who would be the "heirs of salvation" (Hebrews 1:14).

Based on this premise, I can only conclude that all creation is designed to satisfy an infinite God with infinite desires.

The Chief End of Man

Could it be that God went to all this lavish investment of time, material, and lives just to complete His plan and satisfy His desires? This sounds so human!

Precisely! Creator God is not some occluded mystic with whom man cannot identify. The common bond we have with our Maker is the only hope of our own deepest desires being fulfilled and enjoyed forever. No one knows the full extent of all Divine desire, but Jesus told us in simple language, in parables, that a life built on Him is a foundation that will never shift from under our feet, like sand. "For I am the Lord, I do not change" (Malachi 3:6, NKJV). God *is* what He desires, and what He desires never changes. "The fear of the Lord is the beginning of wisdom" (Psalm 111:10, KJV) is the first step toward being really brilliant and really human.

Divine Desires

Jesus spoke in parables to show God's desire for a kingdom that includes the humans He had created.

"The kingdom of heaven is like treasure hidden in a field [Israel], which a man [Jesus/God] found and covered up [by speaking in mysteries]. Then in his joy he goes and sells all that he has and buys that field" (Matthew 13:44, ESV). Divine desire was so great that God gave His only Son to purchase the full redemption of all creation. Mankind, in turn, discovers this kingdom treasure and sells all that he has, making everything subject to this King and His kingdom.

"Again, the kingdom of heaven is like a merchant in search of fine pearls, who, on finding one pearl of great value, went and sold all he had and bought it" (Matthew 13:45–46, ESV). Divine desire for people from all nations is so great that Jesus sends out His Spirit across the earth in every generation, looking for responsive hearts. Anywhere, everywhere there is individual response to the Spirit, the blood of Jesus purchases that soul. The soul in turn who is bought is also like a jeweler looking for rare pearls, who, when he or she finds Jesus, gives all to Him.

Remember that the source of the world's greatest power resides in New Jerusalem and that God's desires are rooted in eternity. His plan for you and for all creation is that everyone would be brought together in His eternal "vessel," His kingdom. The "good" are gathered into the kingdom, while the "bad" are cast outside its walls of safety.

Do you love justice? Do you applaud when you see the "bad guy" finally get apprehended? "So shall it be at the end of the world; the angels shall come forth, and sever the wicked from among the just, and cast them into the furnace of fire: there shall be wailing and gnashing of teeth" (Matthew 13:49–50, KJV). The world systems of political corruption, murder, child abuse, disease, hunger, robbery, terror, and hatred will be vanquished.

"But," you may say, "would God choose that for people He loves, even if they are evildoers?" No, He does not have to. The evildoers punish themselves by their own choice of darkness over light, lies over the truth.

But that is not the way it will end for those who belong to God. For them, God's deepest desires will be fulfilled. Think of life at its most thrilling moment, and then think beyond that and you will catch a glimpse of God's desire: "Eye has not seen, nor ear heard, neither has it entered into the heart of man, the things God has prepared for those who love Him" (1 Corinthians 2:9, JUB).

God is Not Deistic

The world is not a clock that the Clockmaker wound up and then walked away from. We learn from the Old Testament that God desires covenant relationship, not a cohabitation partnership. The compassionate, imaginative Creator wants full interaction with His people.

Has He not said, "I desire mercy [covenant faithfulness], not sacrifice"? God does not accept gifts of diamonds if they come along with unfaithfulness. He will forgive unfaithfulness, but only after genuine repentance. A loving God wants people who *know* Him by intimate experience that is born of desire for Him, His Kingdom, and His ways.

Simply coming up with a formula for creating human bodies is nothing to the Supreme Intelligence. When He creates a life, God conceives it through intimate love that can carry and nurture the human soul to a mature relationship with Him. "[A] time is coming and has now come when the true worshipers will worship the Father in the Spirit and in truth, for they are the kind of worshipers the Father seeks" (John 4:23, NIV).

Divine Desire, Set in Context

In the Garden, God stated the terms for the outworking of His plan: "And I will put enmity between you and the woman, and between your seed and her Seed; He shall bruise your head, and you shall bruise His heel" (Genesis 3:15, NKJV).

When the Word came in human form in Bethlehem, Lucifer observed the activity. A Baby Boy was born; a unique star arose in the night sky; the pounding of camels' hoofs could be heard on the desert floor; Kings from the East bearing gifts could be seen kneeling reverently. Lucifer sensed the pain to his head and he knew the desires of God were advancing on his dark kingdom. But the scene slipped through his fingers until some thirty years later, when he found the Baby Boy, now a full-grown man crying out to the Father. For forty days and nights Lucifer pounded the God-Man with doubts, fears, and an offer of favor: "All the kingdoms of this world I will give you, if you will fall down and worship me" (see Matthew 4:9).

This was Lucifer's final bid before Jesus would suffer the full agony of evil's demonic hosts. Jesus chose between the crumbling cities of the temporary world system and the holy city built on God's eternal values. He chose the holy city, and in the way He did it, He set the pattern for all who will enter His Kingdom. That pattern was one of *sacrifice:* "Whoever finds his life will lose it, and whoever loses his life for my sake will find it" (Matthew 10:39, ESV).

The Conclusion?

Lucifer's goal for the Man-God, the Righteous Man, has been the same in every generation. Since His appearance on earth, Jesus has been mocked, His deity questioned, His name dishonored, His followers ridiculed and martyred, and His resurrection denied. (In 2013, 150,000 Christians were martyred worldwide.) This is the pattern—the injustice of the world system against the righteous. God's desires for all mankind are holy and good, but they are also divisive and permanent. Justice will always convict injustice. History is evidence that, in the end, great cities of the world have nurtured giants of human tragedy, while ignoble little Jerusalem continues to nurture the Messiah, who will come again one day to clean up the rubble and reign in righteousness.

Chapter Three
THE LIFE THAT ENTERS THE KINGDOM

WHAT kind of life enters the Kingdom of God?

To come straight to the point: The *proven life* enters the Kingdom. Jesus is the door, but once a person comes through the door and is inside, God requires a life of covenant faithfulness. The whole biblical narrative is a series of examples of testing for proof. For example:

- Abraham was called to offer his son Isaac.
- Jacob wrestled with the angel for the blessing before He was given the name Israel (Prince of God).
- Joseph was imprisoned for nine years before he was elevated to second in command of Egypt.
- God allowed false prophets and wicked people to live among Israel, to prove them and see if they would follow God. The people of Israel temporarily failed the test.
- Saul (the Apostle Paul) went hungry, was robbed, beaten, imprisoned, maligned, and finally beheaded for bringing the Good News of Jesus to pagans, but he continued to the end.

As Paul wrote, "We must through much tribulation enter into the Kingdom of God" (Acts 14:22, KJV). These are not just generalized, widespread tribulations—each trial is personal. No one else can stand for us; each person must prove him- or herself. In a sense, every obstacle in life is experienced alone, although everyone is surrounded by a host of other people. God set it up this way because He desires a kingdom of people who have passed the test—*overcomers,* not simply comers to the party.

Remember that when Lucifer revolted against the kingdom and brought darkness into the realm of pure light, God, by His Spirit, then pierced that darkness with these words, "Let there be light!" The word "let" means "to become visible." By His wisdom, through the power of His word, God spoke into the darkness, and released light. And God saw that the light was good and beautiful, and He divided the light from the darkness (see Genesis 1:3–4).

Light is beautiful. Good is beautiful. Spiritual identity comes with light and good. Darkness and evil may have an attraction for unproven people, but those who are headed for the Kingdom of God can see darkness for what it is. And should they misstep or get off track, they quickly look to the Light, turn in His direction, and move toward Him until fellowship with the Light is restored.

From the beginning, God recognized no fellowship between darkness and light. Although light must coexist with darkness in this present age, this in no way grants permission for blending, not even on the pretext of witnessing. Believers are the "called out" ones, the ones who witness to the truth in a civil manner, but not while fellowshipping with evil as they do with the family of God. Scripture says:

> For many deceivers have gone out into the
> world, those who do not confess the coming of
> Jesus Christ in the flesh. . . . Watch yourselves,
> so that you may not lose what we have worked
> for. . . . If anyone comes to you and does not bring
> this teaching, do not receive him into your house or
> give him any greeting, for whoever greets him takes
> part in his wicked works. (2 John 7–8, 10, ESV)

Tribulations, Isolation, Cultural Collapse, and Death

How, then, is the church expected to witness, cope with tribulation, and balance the isolation that comes from living in a Luciferian system? Without God, this would be impossible. While each one of us has been made in the likeness of God, we were not made into all-sufficient gods. Being created in the image of God, is not the same as *being* God.

We need to know that the answer to the question, "What kind of people will enter the Kingdom of God?" is this: "people who realize their insufficiency without God." Jesus told his disciples, "Without Me you can do nothing" (John 15:5, NKJV). This is the truth. The all-sufficient God created human beings to be sufficient only through His Son. As Paul wrote to the Philippians: "I can do all things through Christ who strengthens me" (Philippians 4:13, NKJV).

Which is it? Will you be sufficient or insufficient to triumph over all the obstacles in life? You will be whichever you choose! Alone you will die. But with Christ you will live and enter into the eternal kingdom.

Yes, "we enter the kingdom through much tribulation." Yes, each person suffers alone, for him- or herself. And, yes, each person receives the reward for his or her faithfulness as an individual. As Paul wrote:

> Each one will receive his own reward according
> to his own labor. For we are God's fellow workers;
> you are God's field, you are God's building. . . .
> But let each one take heed how he builds on it. . . .
> For no other foundation can anyone lay
> than that which is laid, which is Jesus Christ.
> (1 Corinthians 3:8–9, 11, NKJV)

What Does God Want?

When the history of creation has reached its conclusion and God's ultimate desires are being satisfied, what will the human race look like? If we go back to the image of the egg, and we imagine a baby chick inside the hard shell, slowly pecking its way out of the darkness, we all know that to break the shell from the outside will kill the chick. Through the opposition of the hard shell, the baby chick grows and is strengthened, peck by peck. Finally, the shell breaks into a "new birth," and from there perseveres to maturity. In the human species, we are born of the Spirit, we persevere into manhood, and God receives us into His kingdom as real, bloodline, covenant-keeping sons.

The principle of the seed has been God's way from before the foundations of the world. The earth itself "groans, waiting for the redemption" (see Romans 8:22). Through the process of the seed-planting of truth, followed by opposition, tribulations, struggles great and small, we die to our fallen nature, finally to become sons of the living God. Please read the following carefully with this in mind; Paul answers the question of struggle and death perhaps better than any other writer of Scripture:

> For I consider that the sufferings of the
> present time are not worthy to be compared
> with the glory that is to be revealed to us. For the
> creation was subjected to futility, not willingly, but
> because of him who subjected it, in hope that the
> creation itself will be set free from its bondage to
> corruption and obtain the freedom of the glory of
> the children of God. For we know that the whole
> creation has been groaning together in pains of
> childbirth until now, And not only the creation but
> we ourselves, who have the first fruits of the Spirit,
> groan inwardly as we wait eagerly for adoption
> as sons, the redemption of our bodies. (Romans
> 8:18–23, ESV)

Resurrection! This is the destiny of life with God, spoken in clear language. All creation suffers the storms of opposition to life, until finally, the "natural will" falls into the "soil of surrender" and dies to itself. But to people of the kingdom, resurrection is the next great event. It was *resurrection sons* that God had in mind when He allowed Lucifer to tempt his new humanity. Just as it was God's way when He went into the heart of darkness and began to plant seed of goodness and life into the very heart of darkness and death, so it is His pattern of the Great Commission for all kingdom people—to stand for truth in the midst of a world system of lies and deception.

The Wall of Strength

There is an invisible but very real wall of strength provided for kingdom people. The Spirit of God still hovers over the earth (see Genesis 1:2), with the power to pierce the thick darkness of Egypt, and to part the turbulent waters of the Red Sea. Jesus said "whoever lives and believes in me will never die" (see John 11:26). This is the wall of strength, and it overcomes death. It is an ever-present wall that keeps resurrection at work throughout our life's journey.

The Hypocrite

One of Jesus' names for Lucifer is "hypocrite," which means "a role player." Today, we might call him an "actor." God does not want pretenders, people who play the role of God-worshipers while their hearts remain set on the kingdom of this present age. He does not want a great orator of His Word or a wonderful singer whose goal is self-promotion. God wants those who, when given a choice, choose first His kingdom. These ones are called sons of the Living God, true children of God who will get into His eternal kingdom.

Chapter Four
UNDERSTANDING THE MYSTERY

W HAT does the Bible mean by the word "mysteries"?
Biblical mysteries are the hidden plans of God.
Mysteries are strategically hidden events whose timing and revelation are critical to the fulfillment of God's purposes. As God's mysteries are unveiled, they have an effect on the kingdom of life, the kingdom of darkness, and the natural world.

Sir Isaac Newton, the father of modern science, is reputed to have had one of the greatest minds ever. Yet his scientific exploration of foundational secrets of how creation works, such as his discovery of the law of gravity, was motivated by his desire to discover God and how He works. God is not beyond finding out. His plans are amazingly clear.

Yes, God is invisible. Moses risked his life anyway: "By faith he left Egypt, not being afraid of the anger of the king, for he endured as seeing him who is invisible" (Hebrews 11:23, ESV). Invisible means not perceivable, not non-existent. Although He is invisible to the eyes, hearts and souls crave Him. Through the eyes of his spirit, Moses saw the God "who is Spirit."

God is also omnipotent, but this does not deter us from seeking Him: "For his invisible attributes, namely his eternal power and divine nature, have been clearly perceived, ever since the creation of the world, in the things that have been made" (Romans 1:20, ESV). Both the power and nature of God can be understood through the things we see. The celestial heavens witness to God's superhuman power and His imagination is evidenced by His attention to earthly details of beauty and function. The grandeur of creation provides a daily, worldwide witness of a supreme Designer.

The invisible, omnipotent God is also omniscient. He knows everything, all the time, and his plans always move forward:

> Remember this and stand firm, recall it to mind,
> you transgressors, remember the former things
> of old; for I am God, and there is no other, I am
> God, and there is none like me, declaring the
> end from the beginning. My counsel shall stand,
> and I will accomplish all my purpose. . . . I have
> spoken, and I will bring it to pass; I have purposed,
> and I will do it. (Isaiah 46:8–11, ESV)

God's people can be confident about who God is and what He says about life, as well as confident about the future. The end has already been declared by God through His prophets to Israel, by His Son Jesus, His apostles, and those who know Him, not to mention by the daily preaching of the things that are made.

The Dynamics of Eden

By design, God birthed the human race into the midst of a war; it has always been light versus darkness. The dynamics of Eden were no surprise to God. Lucifer's pride convinced him that he could deceive man and thereby dismantle God's plans, while Adam and Eve were created to star in the first scene of this "cosmic battle," a point which cannot be overstated. The human race has been born into a world of conflict, from small disagreements to major world wars. But that is not the end of the story.

In the ongoing conflict, God is not just crushing rocks; He is creating diamonds under the pressure of opposition: Jesus encouraged his followers with these words: "In the world you will have tribulation; but be of good cheer, I have overcome the world" (John 16:33, NKJV).

Others echoed the same theme:

> Through many tribulations we must enter the
> kingdom of God. (Acts 14:22, ESV)
> I, John, your brother and partner in the
> tribulation and the kingdom and the patient
> endurance that are in Jesus. . . . (Revelation 1:9, ESV)

Human beings do not like to suffer. Every nerve in our natural bodies runs from it, and our minds and emotions respond quickly. Yet we have been clearly warned to expect tribulations—and to see them as a privilege that is given to all citizens of the kingdom. God makes no apology. In Jesus' great high priestly prayer, He said:

> I do not ask that you take them out of the
> world, but that you keep them from the evil one. . . .
> And for their sake I consecrate myself, that they
> may be sanctified [set apart for holy service to
> God], in truth. . . . because you loved me before the
> foundation of the world. (John 17:15, 19, 24, ESV)

Certainly the Father, the Word, and the Holy Spirit—One God— have always enjoyed equal distribution of love. But what caused the Word, who came to Earth in human form, to be designated as the Lamb, not only loved "before the foundation of the world," but also slain before the foundation? Jesus was not simply a good, mortal prophet, Jesus was the Word of God. He created all things, and He fulfilled all righteousness, even to death on the cross.

Mysteries Prepared Before the Foundation of the World

I discover in Scripture what I saw in visionary form—a beautiful, luminescent kingdom with a city. The visions reveal many mysteries along the lines of what Paul wrote to the church at Corinth, "among the mature we do impart wisdom, although it is not a wisdom of this age or of the rulers of this age, who are doomed to pass away. But we impart a secret and hidden wisdom of God, which God decreed before the ages for our glory" (1 Corinthians 2:6–7, ESV).

"Our glory"? Before the creation of our world God was thinking about what would bring you and me glory? That is what Scripture reveals:

> But as it is written, "what no eye has seen,
> nor ear heard, nor the heart of man imagined,
> what God has prepared for those who love him."
> (1 Corinthians 2:9, ESV)
>
> Then the King will say to those on his right, "Come, you who are blessed by my Father, inherit the kingdom prepared for you from the foundation of the world." (Matthew 25:34, ESV)
>
> Blessed be the God and Father of our Lord Jesus Christ, who has blessed us in Christ with every spiritual blessing in the heavenly places, even as he chose us in him before the foundation of the world, that we should be holy and blameless before him. (Ephesians 1:3–4, ESV)
>
> By faith in Christ, we are counted blameless, sinless, forgiven in the sight of God, worthy of citizenship in the glorious heavenly city.

The Good Shepherd

Using the metaphor of the shepherd and sheep, Jesus said,

> I am the door of the sheep. All [religious leaders] who ever came before Me [or after me] are thieves and robbers, but the sheep did not hear them. . . . The thief does not come except to steal, and to kill, and to destroy [the eternal soul]. I have come that they may have life, and that they may have it more abundantly. I am the good shepherd. The good shepherd gives His life for the sheep. . . . I am the good shepherd; and I know My sheep, and am known by My own. (John 10:7–8, 10–11, 14, NKJV)

This is yet another way of stating the single greatest revelation of the eight visions: The Father and the Good Shepherd are One God. The Word of God came out from God and was God. What religious leader was with Father God before creation? What religious leader created the universe? Shed his blood to cover the sins of all penitents, of whatever ethnicity? What religious leader promised eternal life in the eternal kingdom of God? Only Jesus.

Chapter Five

IS LUCIFER/SATAN A REAL BEING?

I S Lucifer/Satan a real being? From what I saw in the visions and understand in Scripture, Lucifer was once the highest of the archangels. Far from being like the foolish devil caricature in a red suit with a pitchfork, Lucifer's is one of the highest intelligences ever created by God. The number of angels under his command numbers in the millions. He was certainly the most beautiful, impressive creation I saw in the visions.

Lucifer's first departure from God started with a single thought: coveting what God was creating for himself (breaking the tenth commandment). Following this thought, his primary motivation was to become ruler of this newly-created world, with the goal of receiving the praise and worship of its inhabitants, the worship that only God deserves. To achieve this position, Lucifer took his one-third of the angelic host (the ones over which he ruled), and placed them in rank as principalities, powers, and rulers of the darkness of this age. It seems that common angels were assigned the demonic works of terrorizing and afflicting the bodies and the minds of people with physical ailments, diseased ideologies, and false religious doctrines. (See Ephesians 6:12.)

According to Job 2:1, along with other passages of Scripture, although Lucifer has lost his heavenly excellencies, he is still allowed to appear before the divine council with legal accusations against the people of God. He is called "the accuser of the brethren." This tells us that heaven is not a fluffy place for vaporous beings with nothing to do, rather it is the vortex of world government.

Everything about the Spirit realm is governed by superhuman power. Both heaven and earth reveal cosmic powers that defy human comprehension. If we look back to Vision Seven, where the "Arm of the Lord" is revealed, we will be able to understand the magnitude of the final battle that is looming between Lucifer and King Messiah.

A battle is coming between Lucifer and his old friend, the archangel Michael, that will exile Lucifer from heaven altogether. Knowing that he has "but a short time," Lucifer will advance from a war on Israel to her offspring the Church and finally to King Messiah, at Armageddon, where he will be bound and cast into sheol for a thousand years, awaiting his final sentencing in the lake of fire.

Is this Lucifer simply an illusion or a cute little mascot for someone who wants to be naughty? Correspondingly, is evil only imagined or taught? Are lies harmless? What about killing? Stealing? Destruction? Terror? Do some human beings commit brutal, inhumane acts? Is death real? Have governments historically been corrupt? Where does the oppression of humankind originate, if not with Lucifer?

The world is beautiful. Nature is intelligently designed. Human beings can be great builders of life on planet Earth, creative, imaginative, helpful, caring, loving, and family oriented. Human beings are worshipers. The only way to explain the difference between these two aspects of the world is to use the words, "good" and "evil."

I take the word of Jesus—the *Arm of God*—who created all things and who will bring down every power-hungry government that has oppressed mankind. I take the word of Him who will rule the Earth with justice and equity. I take the word of Him whose words will never be dropped from the eternal lexicon. I take the word of Jesus, who declared that Lucifer/Satan will be cast out of heaven permanently. I take the word of the Word.

Lucifer is real and he will fall. The dark angel's own evil will one day roll back upon him in a real lake of fire prepared from his own flaming desires. Then at last, Earth will be cleansed of its suffering, safe from harm, and abounding in peace.

Chapter Six
THE ETERNAL KINGDOM

THE eternal Kingdom is the rule of God established over all other intelligences in creation. The Creator God chose to enter into creation as Sovereign, whereby He both reigns and interacts with all that He has made.

The last great war of the world will be a cosmic battle to finalize the legal issue between God and Lucifer concerning Lucifer's role in eternity. On one side will be Lucifer's army of angels and the people who will have followed him; on the other side will be God's army of angels and the people who will have followed Him.

The great warrior David wrote of God's angelic army:

> Bless the Lord, O you his angels,
> You mighty ones who do his word,
> Obeying the voice of his word!
> Bless the Lord, all His hosts,
> His ministers who do his will!
> (Psalm 103:20–21, ESV)

David understood that it takes God and his angels to settle cosmic issues. Wars have always been settled by heaven's decree. According to Isaiah, "Bel [an idol, a false god] bows down" (Isaiah 46:1), along with all who follow his system:

> At the name of Jesus every knee should bow,
> of things in heaven, and things in earth, and things
> under the earth; And that every tongue confess that

Jesus Christ [the form I saw emerging out of the flame of Father God] is Lord to the glory of God the Father. (Philippians 2:10–11, ESV)

Back to the Garden

The Kingdom of Heaven ruled the Garden of Eden. The day God explained to Adam that one tree was forbidden, He revealed that Eden was under heaven's government. But with their own free will at work along with the deception of Lucifer's subversive counsel, the man and woman eventually violated the law of God, which precipitated the struggle for dominion in which we live today. The first couple was dispelled from the Garden, followed by a heartbreaking murder and exile of their son. The endless cycle of wars and human cruelty had begun, but God never left His creation for a moment. His strategy had already been planned *before the foundations of the earth were laid*. Eventually there would be a final battle that would "end all wars," identified by God as the "War of Crushing the Head," which is what He declared to Lucifer after the Fall of the man and the woman. The "Seed" of the woman would crush Lucifer's head. (See Genesis 3:15.)

After several thousand years, Earth time, God prepared a body and planted that divine Seed into the womb of a virgin in Nazareth named Mary. Mary was of the royal blood line of King David, and so was her husband Joseph. The Seed had every legal right to be King of the Jews, naturally speaking. But as the divine Seed prepared by God, He had every right to assume the throne of the Kingdom of Heaven on earth.

In human form, Jesus submitted to the cross, suffered physically and died, descended into the lower regions of earth, confronted Lucifer, and won the rights to planet Earth, legally and literally. However He still had the duty of building His Called out Ones and rescuing Israel. Resurrected and returned to heaven—where, in visionary form, I saw Him as the Arm of the Lord, and then in full bodily form. Until He returns to assume the throne of David, Jesus is actively advocating for the saints on earth. For several thousand years, the Kingdom of Heaven has been advancing the kingdom system and expanding the holy city. As literally as the Seed came the first time, He will return and complete His taking of the full possession of all nations and peoples.

All non-biblical religions come from Lucifer-inspired philosophy. Without spiritual enlightenment, distortions of spiritual realities have blinded the majority of every generation and molded entire cultures around false gods, ideologies, and political systems that are destined to be destroyed. But in spite of satanic revolutions and crumbled empires, the Kingdom of Heaven has continued to increase its population.

Proof of Lucifer's failures are as old as human history. Instead of proving that his dark kingdom is what mankind needs, his deceptions have produced one long cry of human suffering. In the vision, I watched the great fire of God blast the entire army of Lucifer into the atmosphere, where they disappeared with one command! Dissatisfied over the loss of what he considered a better position, Satan was also dismissed from Mount Zion, never to sit in the honored counsels again. Now he can only stand in the gallery, as the accuser of believers.

The Kingdom Is Near

But when Jesus was born as King of the Jews, His ministry on Earth began with a call to repentance, "for the kingdom of heaven is at hand" (see Matthew 3:2).

And He warned His people about obsessions with the temporary things of this age when He said, "Seek ye first the Kingdom of God and his righteousness, and all these [natural] things will be added unto you" (Matthew 6:33, KJV). All human systems and governments are coming to a close. Even the world admits to this. In 1990, Trends Research Institute published an article in the *Boston Globe* asserting that "all systems are breaking down worldwide." Their prediction is proving to be true.

Active Participation Required

On one occasion Jesus told a parable about three men who were given talents (money). Out of fear, one man hid his talent. When his master returned he took that man's one talent and gave it to the person with ten talents. Jesus then revealed a kingdom mystery, "For to everyone who has will more be given and he will have abundance" (Matthew 25:29, NKJV).

Large or small, the kingdom principle is based on the law of use. Using what you have been given has great reward. Failure to use your talents is rebellion and will impoverish you for eternity.

As John wrote in his visions, the kingdoms of this world are about to change hands: "Then the seventh angel sounded: and there were great voices in heaven, saying, The kingdoms of this world have become the kingdoms of our Lord, and of his Christ; and he shall reign forever and ever" (Revelation 11:15, NKJV).

Chapter Seven
SUMMATION

A S we come to a summary of the visions, the question may be posed once again: "So, what's the point?"

Think of a cup of coffee with cream. Once it has been thoroughly stirred, the two substances become inseparable. There is a word in Greek, *katallasso,* which describes this mutual blending together to form a different compound. In the English Bible, this word means "to reconcile." *A person whose life has been reconciled to God has been changed into a different person.* The old, human nature has died and the new divine nature now rules the heart, mind, and spirit of the person. The kingdom is not present in a person's human nature, but once that person has received the divine nature— the nature of God given through spiritual birth—the kingdom has come.

In Jesus' high priestly prayer for His followers, He shows this blending together with God: ". . . that they [believers] may all be one, just as you, Father, are in me, and I in you, that they also may be in us, so that the world may believe that you have sent me. . . and loved them as you have loved me" (John 17:21, 23, ESV).

Fallen human nature can be changed into the image of God. Before the foundations of the earth were laid, this was the plan: to have a kingdom of holy people, from His own blood, whose hearts and lives were blended with His.

A Review of the Visions

In brief summary, let us take one last review:

In Vision One, I saw the Kingdom of God, the city of New Jerusalem, and a civilization of angels who were occupied in various kinds of work and in the worship of God. We learned that only God is omniscient, and that angels living in the kingdom understand only what is revealed to them.

Whereas angels were the first to be created and live in God's kingdom, once mankind was created and entered into covenant with Him, the mysteries of God's plans began to unfold on earth. The "church in the wilderness" began with the people of the first covenant, Israel, and the New Covenant with Israel and Judah that expanded to all people, which includes believing Gentiles from all nations and languages.

In the present age, angels observe the Church for greater understanding of these mysteries. The Apostle Paul wrote:

> For this reason I, Paul, a prisoner for Christ
> Jesus on behalf of you Gentiles . . . how the
> mystery was made known to me by revelation . . .
> the mystery of Christ, which was not made known
> in other generations as it has now been revealed
> to his holy apostles and prophets by the Spirit . . .
> and to bring to light to everyone what is the plan
> of the mystery hidden for ages in God who created
> all things, so that through the church the manifold
> wisdom of God might be made known to the rulers
> and authorities in the heavenly places. (Ephesians
> 3:1, 2–5, 9–10, ESV)

What an honor! What a responsibility! As a believer, you are being observed by angels, anxious to learn the mysteries of the kingdom that have been hidden to them since before the creation of the earth. When we believers gather to worship or study God's word, angels are looking over our shoulders, eager to learn more about Jesus.

In Vision Two, the archangels Michael, Gabriel, and Lucifer were called to the presence of God, in preparation for a great announcement.

In Vision Three, the archangels informed their captains to pass on the word—God was about to address the entire population of angels. This scene reveals the intense desire of angels to hear from God.

In Vision Four, all angels were present and spontaneous worship erupted, with sounds of ecstasy beyond human description. The endless heavens were filled with a luminescent glow. Lucifer took the lead in this worship, with Michael and Gabriel following.

Music is a great part of God's world. Scientists tell us that atoms emit sound. Stars sing. Songs of the redeemed are being sung around the throne of God today, and at King Jesus' return we will all sing the songs of Moses, the beautiful Psalms of David, and others whose names we may have never heard.

("Songs of the Lord," songs birthed by the Holy Spirit, lift the soul and heal the brokenness of our lives. In a church where I was on staff, we had an outpouring of Holy Spirit inspiration where new songs were sung spontaneously in every service for approximately five years. One evening a deaf woman stood and sang a new song from her heart to God—not in perfect pitch, but in purity of spirit, and there were no dry eyes in the house. By the end of that special period, thousands of such songs filled twenty song books; and produced numerous recordings. It was a taste of what the angels experience in the presence of God. Spirit-birthed music heals the soul, while the music of the fallen worship-leading archangel Lucifer destroys the moral structure of nations and entire cultures.)

In Vision Five the "day of announcement" arrived. As God spoke, the sky became like an Omni theater. We might call it the opening scene of *The Celestial Creation Story*. It was awesome to watch the images of the coming creation appearing on heaven-wide screen. There was great celebration among the angels, joined by images of people from every nation and language worshiping God! (Remember, humanity had not even been created at that point.) It was a foretaste of the day when "everything that has breath" praises the Lord.

In Vision Six we saw the consequences of free will—the freedom to choose or reject God. This choice is the only real freedom available to mankind. Every moment of life on earth is framed by the results of these two choices. Pure freedom of human nature is a myth. Man only has freedom to choose or reject God. All people worship; the question is, who receives that worship?

The great archangel Lucifer chose to worship himself. In doing so, he exchanged the excellencies of heaven for eternal condemnation—taking with him one-third of the angels. The choice remains open until the kingdom comes in full array and brings human choice to an end.

In Vision Seven we joined with the archangels for a glimpse of the manifestation of the "Arm of the Lord." To see the Arm of the Lord, the very emblem of power, coming out of the light of the Eternal One with lightning-like force, stirs the deepest soul and causes the scales to fall from the undiscerning eyes. This was creation's first glimpse of "the Word in bodily form." "Say therefore to the people of Israel, I am the Lord, and I will bring you out from under the burdens . . . and I will redeem you with an outstretched arm, and with great acts of judgment" (Exodus 6:6, ESV).

In Vision Eight is where I saw the great "outstretched Arm" come into His complete bodily form. Following this revelation of the "Word in bodily form," Lucifer's revolt was exposed and condemned. Light pierced the darkness and the earth took up its orbit, seeded with life. When the Seed was announced, Lucifer's defeat became certain. This was the infancy of God's desire for a covenant-faithful humanity which would eventually accomplish all that He purposed. Death would come, but life would prevail until humanity was transformed into the image of God.

Here, in outline is a synopsis of the mysteries:

- God's first work of creation was the heavens—space, wisdom, angels, the Holy City.
- Angelic rebellion occurred. Darkness appeared, then was dispelled.

- Light pierced the darkness; Earth was created.
- Celestial lights were created in the second heavens.
- Earth was seeded with life and humanity.
- The six-day Creation was finished.
- The seventh day was a day of rest.
- Lucifer entered the Garden.
- Humanity rebelled against God.
- Abraham and his descendents were called to produce the Seed—the Messiah.
- Messiah (the Man-Ruler) was born, announced the kingdom, was crucified for sin, was resurrected, promised to return.
- The King is coming back to Jerusalem, Israel, to rule the nations.
- The millennial kingdom of God will arrive, followed by one thousand years of peace and restoration.
- The white throne judgment of the lost will take place.
- Lucifer and his host will be cast into the lake of fire.
- New Jerusalem will come down. Immanuel, God, will be with humanity forever.
- Eternity.

"The kingdoms of this world have become the kingdoms of our Lord and of His Christ, and He shall reign forever and ever" (Revelation 11:15, NKJV).

Holding Onto Reality

Social engineers are working in concert to rewrite literal history into their understanding of today's reality. In their new reality, literal history is irrelevant and disconnected from today's world, and reality should only be defined by the present. It is a move that is already evidenced through the devolving family and influence of the Church. The biblical God is being redefined by non-biblical religious systems.

Without doubt, one of the primary reasons I was allowed to see what happened before our world was created was to trumpet the *reality* of God and His intentions. According to definition: the principle of reality is a law given to enable mankind to "defer immediate instinctual gratification in order to achieve long-range goals." In other words, it is unrealistic to live by the instinct for immediate satisfaction. A wise today can only be built on a real yesterday in light of a real tomorrow.

Reality is what actually exists. God exists. You and I exist, and everything man does, says, or thinks has future consequences. No sane person lives only in the moment. Time is always present, but our moment in time has been sequenced into past, present, and future.

Two Witnesses

I saw the Holy City in visionary form, yet we have evidence of its existence by two clear witnesses. Jerusalem above and Jerusalem on earth are the two witnesses that give physical evidence to the realities portrayed in the biblical text. Jerusalem is written about extensively in the Bible, and, except Jerusalem, no other earthly city in human history is known to have a heavenly counterpart.

Jerusalem is the most controversial city on earth. No other city compares with its ability to throw the entire world into war at the least offence.

From the beginning, God put His signature on this particular spot of earth for himself. Judah (the Jews) would possess the land (see Genesis 49:9), and the House of David would be its throne-keeper (see 2 Samuel 5), when King Messiah comes to assume world government:

> The angel Gabriel was sent from God to a city
> of Galilee . . . to a virgin betrothed to a man whose
> name was Joseph, of the house of David. . . . "Do not
> be afraid, Mary, for you have found favor with God.
> And behold, you will conceive in your womb and
> bear a son, and you shall call his name Jesus. He will
> be great and will be called Son of the Most High. And

the Lord God will give to him the throne of his father
David, he will reign over the house of Jacob forever,
and of his kingdom there will be not end." (Luke
1:26–27, 30–33, ESV)

This reality is confirmed thirty years later by the Apostle John
who wrote:

And I saw the holy city, new Jerusalem coming
down out of heaven from God, as a bride adorned
for her husband. And I heard a loud voice from the
throne saying, "Behold, the dwelling place of God
is with man. He will dwell with them, and they will
be his people, God himself will be with them as
their God." (Revelation 21:2–3, ESV)

Long before John's message, Zechariah wrote:

Sing and rejoice, O daughter of Zion, for
behold, I come and I will dwell in your midst,
declares the Lord. And many nations [Gentiles]
shall join themselves to the Lord in that day, and
shall be my people. And I will dwell in your midst,
and you shall know that the Lord of hosts has sent
me to you. And the Lord will inherit Judah as his
portion in the holy land, and will again choose
Jerusalem. Be silent, all flesh, before the Lord,
for he has roused himself from his holy dwelling.
(Zechariah 2: 10–13, ESV)

Before the beginning of our world, there was God. We exist
because of Him. At the end of human governments and systems,
there will be God, and He will bring down His kingdom city–the
city for which Abraham looked, the city about which Luke, John, and
Zechariah wrote, the city I was blessed to catch a glimpse of, and from
that city He will live among His people forever. Emmanuel–God with
us. The future will see His glory!

Chapter Eight
A PREVIEW

THERE is more to come beyond what I have shared in this book. Though it has not come in visionary form, new understanding continues to flow, accompanied by a wealth of tearful amazement at the reality of a Creator who has actually declared himself in human form, and laid out His plans at the cost of His life and the lives of tens of thousands of His followers. I am stunned to find that the Book of Genesis is, in a sense, an autobiography of God. The majority of our theological and scientific debates about creation have been absorbed in trying to satisfy our intellectual curiosity, at the expense of discovering the greater spiritual realities of who God is.

As we came to the close of completing this book on the visions, God took me once again to the story of Adam and Eve. The revelation I received will be chapter one of my next book, but I want to share with you a glimpse of what Moses wrote in the book of Genesis. What I have learned will provide many answers for the questioning heart and intellect.

A Glimpse Into God's Story

God said, "I declare the end from the beginning" (see Isaiah 46:9–10). The first priority of the Book of Genesis is to tell God's story, of which mankind is a part. The world is God-centric, not man-centered. "In the beginning God," signals the mind to turn its focus Godward. To correctly understand the controversial book of Genesis, we must look first for God in every detail of its unfolding story.

It is commonly held that the Book of Genesis contains "good stories that make a good point." While this is true, to see it only as good stories is both infantile and tragic, even deadly. Human history is approaching its final conclusion, and this is "the end" to which God refers when He said He declares "the end from the beginning." It is the end of human history, not the end of God's creation which will never pass away.

To a depth partially veiled to our forefathers, God is unveiling himself and His eternal plans to this generation. Both the wise and the unwise have crossed the stage of humanity for thousands of years, as the story has been unfolding, but the closer we get to the conclusion, the more we understand and the more we need to understand. The closer you get to the end of a book or film, the better you will understand what has been taking place throughout the story—if you have been paying attention.

Pairs are the pattern of life, from the principle of action/reaction to the fact that all creature-life was created in pairs. Then why did God make Adam alone? He himself said, "it is not good that man should be alone" (Genesis 2:18, NKJV). Then why did He do it?

God made Adam alone. God is telling us His story through the creation account. He began alone. Revealing to us through Adam that "it is not good to be alone," it is through a glorious plan that He is making one compatible to himself.

Two Adams

In actual fact, in God's story there are two Adams. The first Adam was a prototype of the last Adam, the head of the human race, which is why his sin affected all of natural mankind (created from the dust). The last Adam is also the head of a race, the new man created in the image and likeness of the last Adam from heaven—(the man planted into the womb of Mary.) (See Ephesians 2:14-16; 4:23-23; and Colossians 3:9-11.) "The first man Adam became a living being; the last Adam became a life-giving spirit. But it is not the spiritual that is first but the natural, and then the spiritual. The first man was from the dust; the second man is from heaven" (1 Corinthians 15:45–47, ESV).

God celebrated all of His creatures, but none fulfilled His desire (which is like the first Adam, who could not find a suitable companion). The first Adam portrayed God's desire for covenant relationships. And then we see that God gave the first Adam a companion:

> So the Lord God caused a deep sleep to fall upon the man, and while he slept he took one of his ribs and closed up its place with flesh. And the rib that the Lord God had taken from the man he made into a woman and brought her to the man. Then the man said, "This at last is bone of my bones and flesh of my flesh; she shall be called Woman, because she was taken out of Man."
> (Genesis 2:21–22, ESV)

The woman, Eve, was not created from the dust of the earth, as was Adam and all animals, but with greater honor, she was taken from Adam's own body. She was "bone of his bone and flesh of his flesh," beautiful, beloved, and called to a covenant relationship. "Therefore shall a man leave his father and mother and the two shall become one flesh" (Genesis 2:24, NKJV).

But Lucifer/Satan came into the Garden and initiated his plot to stop the plan that God had displayed before all the angels in heaven on the day of the great announcement. Eve was God's prize, a type of all covenant believers from every generation—God's beloved. Therefore, with adultery in his heart, Satan actually determined to take God's prize for himself.

The Plan

But God, always light years ahead of Lucifer/Satan, knew how it would work out. Suffering lay ahead for the human race, but so did glory. Just as the first Adam had became a living being, so the last

Adam, who was yet to come on the scene, would become a life-giving Spirit. The parallels are plain:

First Adam:

> God caused a deep sleep to come upon Adam.
> He surgically opened his side and
> removed a rib.
> He closed the wound and created Eve out
> of the body of Adam.
> He woke him up then presented his
> beautiful covenant partner, Eve, to him.

Last Adam:

> On the Cross, His side was pierced, out came
> blood and water.
> God caused a deep sleep (physical death) to
> come upon Jesus.
> On the third day Jesus arose from the
> grave. His new creation bride rose with Him.
> The Covenant Saints await their presentation
> to King Messiah, Jesus—which will come at the
> "marriage supper of the Lamb."

The story of the first Adam and Eve explains God's loving plan and desire for a people in covenant relationship with Him. The last Adam and Eve are King Messiah and His Holy City of Saints that are coming down to live and reign on the earth.

The praise and worship have already begun. Is it any wonder that John "heard, as it were, the voice of a great multitude, and as the voice of many waters, and as the voice of mighty thunderings, saying, Hallelujah! for the Lord God Omnipotent reigns!" (Revelation 19:6, NKJV).